Fort Wayne's Trolleys

HORSE CARS
STREET CARS
INTERURBANS
TROLLEY COACHES
MOTOR BUSES

1870 — 1963

Fort Wayne's

Trolleys

GEORGE K. BRADLEY

OWEN DAVIES, PUBLISHER   CHICAGO, ILLINOIS

Fort Wayne's Trolleys

Copyright© 1963

by George Kitching Bradley.

Published by

Owen Davies

1214 North LaSalle Street - Chicago, Illinois

Printed in the United States of America by Keefer Printing Co., Fort Wayne, Indiana

Library of Congress Catalog - Card No. 63-21978

1st Printing   November, 1963

TO DAD,

Who always had time to wait for one more train or answer one more question, pleasing a small boy.

Acknowledgments

Swift motor buses glide through the streets of Fort Wayne and little remains to suggest the once comprehensive electric railway and streetcar system that served the city. Occasionally, a rail can be seen peering from the pavement in the city and in the country grass-covered embankments remain as reminders of the interurban lines that radiated in five directions. These are now milestones in the distinguished ninety year history of Fort Wayne's modern transit system.

If this history had been undertaken before 1947, much valuable information, now lost forever, might have been easily gathered. Unfortunately, in the seperation of the power and transit facilities a large amount of data was destroyed as it had no current value. No comprehensive study of the company had ever been compiled and no complete history has ever been written. As many available sources as possible were used for this history.

The fine co-operation of many individuals should not go unrecognized. Foremost of these is Mr. Donald H. Walker, President of the progressive Fort Wayne Transit, Inc., who originally proposed the gathering together of all the facts of the firm's history. Herb Harnish aided in gathering details and is responsible for ninety percent of the photographic reproductions. Many of these were rescued from badly faded prints. Mr. E. A. Luhman and the Indiana & Michigan Electric Company generously loaned old records and furnished statistics. The Fort Wayne Public Library staff was most helpful and patient in the use of newspaper micro-films. Mr. Roy M. Bates, local historian, gave considerable valuable help as did Mr. Daniel Reibel, present director, and Mr. Richard Haupt, former director, of the Allen County - Fort Wayne Historical Society.

Many others contributed information and gave invaluable aid which has been much appreciated. The following individuals were kind enough to provide pictures, augmenting those already in the Bradley - Harnish Collection. However, as the same pictures were, in some cases, received from different persons, individual photo credits are not given.

O. F. Lee
Stanley Johnson
Sidney Pepe
Paul Willer
Malcolm MacCarter
Harry Zillmer

Glen Nicely
James F. Cook
J. W. Greenland
Barry Neuberger
Eugene Van Dusen
George Krambles

Historical Society of Pennsylvania

Contents

1   Citizens' Horsecars 1870   9
2   The Magic of Electricity 1892   17
3   Splendid Robison Park 1896   21
4   Wabash Valley Interurban Empire 1900   27
5   The Lean Teens 1913   43
6   The Indiana Service Corporation 1920   51
7   A Completely Modern Street Railway
       1920-1931   63
8   The Spy Run Plant   75
9   Thirty Changing Years 1932-1962   83
10   The Small City Lines   99
11   Rolling Stock   105
12   Statistics   149
      Notes   170
      Bibliography   172
      Index   173

Citizens' Horsecars

When the Civil War period ended, Fort Wayne was definitely the commercial center of northeastern Indiana. A crossroad since earliest times, transportation was firmly established with good connections to other areas by canal, railroad, and plank roads. Modes of transportation constantly change and the Wabash and Erie Canal was a dying institution as the steel rails continued to move across the land. Within the rapidly growing city, public transit was virtually non-existant. The only such attempt had been an omnibus line to connect the rail depot with the Rockhill House situated near the canal at Broadway and Main.[1] This line was primarily for the benefit of this hostelry and was short lived. The public press clamored for an efficient and comprehensive transit system.

On September 8, 1871, a group of leading citizens, including J. H. Bass, S. T. Hanna, S. B. Bond and G. E. Bursley, met to solve this situation by forming the Citizens' Street Railroad Company with a capitalization of $50,000.[2] These men knew that the venture was of paramount importance to the growth and future of Fort Wayne. They went before the City Council with a proposal to lay rails from Main and Calhoun south to Creighton Avenue then west to Fairfield Avenue and also east from Calhoun on Wallace Street to Hanna Street.[3] It was no chance coincidence that the owners had business and land interests in the areas to be served.

The permission granted, contractors began to work in earnest on the tracks of the Citizens' Street Railroad Company. Two small horsecars arrived in the opening days 1872 and these, the accepted type of transit vehicle, were to be the curtain raisers on the city transportation scene. On January 6, 1872, at 3:45 P.M., city engineer Charles Breckenridge and company president John H. Bass drove the first car over Calhoun Street to the Aveline House where a huge celebration was held to toast the progress of the community. Many people now felt Fort Wayne had arrived as a metropolitan area equal to any city.[4]

The first two cars were immediately joined by two more and the company became a paying proposition. Two more lines were built east and west from Main and Calhoun streets where the company offices were located. The east line turned south on Lafayette to Jefferson while the west line turned south on Broadway also terminating at Jefferson.[5] A turntable was built in the middle of the Main and Calhoun intersection to avoid costly switches and allow quick turnarounds. By the fall the east line had been extended on Jefferson to Maumee Road.

Before the first year was over, the company suffered from a national malady; "The Great Epizootic," which was an epidemic of influeza in horses. All large stables were excellent targets for the temporaryily disabling disease and the company's Chestnut Street stable and barns were no exception. Service was irregular during November and December with a complete suspension from November 23 to December 4. The cars then began running with mules doing part of the pulling until the horses recovered, but Sunday service was temporarily ended.

Undaunted by this setback, the company continued to expand with extended trackage and more cars. In July 1874, track was built on Jefferson Street west from Broadway to Garden Street and the new Fairgrounds while the east line was extended north on Harmer and east on Washington to Glasgow Avenue.[6] Eight cars were in regular daily service in 1876, although it is believed the company owned ten, numbered 10 through 19. Shortly afterwards a curious newcomer appeared in Fort Wayne in the form of the Jenny Electric Light Company with a Mr. Ronald T. McDonald as manager, but at this time no logical connection could be seen be-

Citizens' Street Railroad #14 at Jefferson and Broadway during the "80's". The conductor wears a high crowned hat, which was the standard instead of the uniform cap.

Citizens' Street R. R. #16 turning from Jefferson onto Broadway, about 1885.

tween this firm and the horsecars.

The Citizens' Street Railroad took progressive measures to improve service but one such attempt, to avoid being stuck in the snow, was threatened by the editors of the Fort Wayne Sentinel in this gem of nearsighted wisdom: "No sooner did the snow begin to fall this morning than the street car employees began to scatter salt broadcast on Calhoun Street. This is the way sleighing is spoiled on the main thoroughfare and businessmen cut off from their trade. How long will the authorities permit this outrage?" [7]

On March 1, 1873, to raise expansion capital, the company had executed a $20,000 mortgage upon all its properties and rights. During the succeeding years they neglected to pay off the mortgage and also defaulted on the original bonds. The result was a court case in March 1887 and a change of venue was demanded to move the case out of Allen County. The court action finally landed in the Noble County Circuit Court. In this interim period the company was placed in receivership with Mr. Sidney Lumbard appointed receiver.[8]

Prior to 1887, all the carlines were south of the St. Mary's and Maumee rivers as the County Commissioners were reluctant to let the cars cross the bridges. During the summer of 1887 the Citizens' Company, on petition of the receiver, and with court permission, was allowed to lay tracks over the Wells Street Bridge to tap suburban Bloomingdale. Tracks started at Main and Calhoun, went north to Superior, and west to Wells. North of the river the new line was built on Cass Street to Third Street and west to Wells. This new construction followed the double tracking of Calhoun Street in the previous year.[9]

The receivership was terminated and the company sold, on orders of the court, to satisfy all outstanding claims. The company was sold at the court house door, on August 13, 1887, for $110,000 to J. H. Bass and S. B. Bond.[10] These two gentlemen and Mr. Frank DeH. Robinson formed the Fort Wayne Street Railroad Company on August 22, 1887, capitalized at $300,000. The three each held nine hundred ninety-nine, one hundred dollar shares. The remaining three were held by J. M. Barrett and A. S. Bond. This was rather handsome profit for Bass and Bond as they sold their rights in the existing street railway to the new company for $391,000, mostly in stock.[11]

This event marked the beginning of a series of corporate title scrambles that would continue for the next fifty years. The re-organized company immediately purchased nineteen new horse-cars and projected further expansions.

During the same summer, Mr. C. L. Centlivre of the C. L. Centlivre Brewing Company decided to build a car line through the Riverside area north to his brewery. Most of this area was not inside the city and the permission of the County Commissioners was necessary. They allowed him to build north on Spy Run Avenue, from the St. Mary's River bridge, to the brewery, but not to cross the old bridge. The line ended at the canal bridge three blocks south of Cent-

Fort Wayne Street Railroad #16, purchased in 1888. This was the second car with the number 16.

livre Park, the company owned beer garden. Then, as now, Indiana county commissioners had jurisdiction over river and stream bridges whether inside a municipality or not. Motive power was no problem for the new venture as the brewery already had horses available and the line was opened on August 14th. The C. L. Centlivre Street Railway ran with a three block gap between it and the other city lines until late in the summer of 1888 when they were allowed to lay tracks across the new Spy Run Avenue bridge and run their horse cars to Superior and Calhoun.[12]

The year 1888 saw the Fort Wayne Street Railroad make some notable improvements. By extending the Broadway line south to Creighton and then east to the existing line at Fairfield the "Belt Line" was created. At this time Creighton Avenue was, roughly, the southern boundary of the city and Broadway was very close to the western edge. The name Belt Line stuck although in later years it only encircled the southwestern commercial district. This was the only circular line in the city and the only one to operate cars in both directions. The Hanna Street line was also extended from the Wallace and Hanna terminus to John Street, then south to Creighton and east to Walton Avenue, now Anthony Boulevard. The West Main line was created by building west from Broadway to the city limits at the Leesburg Road.[13] This line terminated at the gates of the well kept and spacious grounds of Lindenwood Cemetery. Cemeteries in all cities seemed to be a good traffic generator and the new West Main was no exception. The street railway was expanding with the city.

The turntable, located in the center of the city's main intersection, became an obsolete nuisance and a source of some irritation to the public, as each car had to wait its opportunity

East Main from Calhoun Street, showing one of Fort Wayne Street Rys. horse cars, probably from the second series.

Centlivre Street Railway Company #5 on Spy Run Avenue. It is not known whether these cars regularly carried a conductor.

to turn or cross. The turntable was removed on November 15, 1888 and replaced with special trackwork, allowing the cars to turn or pass through with relatively little effort. Main and Calhoun was still the principal transfer point for all lines and the "turntable corner" became the "Transfer Corner", a name carried to this day.

The first storage barn and stable had been built by the Citizens' company in 1872, east of Calhoun on the north side of Chestnut Street. The name of the street was changed several times which creates some confusion. In 1910, Chestnut became Carl Street but, in 1929, it was changed again, this time to Baker Street.[14] In the early days it was refered to as the Chestnut or South Barns, but in later years simply called Baker Street. The Chestnut Barn area was enlarged by the purchase of much of the property on the south side of the street, through to Railroad Street. The Pennsylvania depot built by the Pittsburg, Fort Wayne and Chicago was just across Railroad Street. The first brick stable burned in 1884 at a loss of $7,000, but was replaced with a much larger brick structure, a block long between Chestnut and Breckenridge Streets. Part of this site had been occupied by the Episcopal Church of the Good Shepherd. A large, sheet metal, six track car barn stood next to the stable.

The east side of Fort Wayne was experiencing considerable growth at this time and the company elected to build another barn at the northwest corner of Washington and Glasgow, on the city limits. At the time, 1888, this seemed to be a reasonable and logical location however time would prove it to be the worst possible choice and a nearly isolated location. The "East Barns" included a stable that housed one hundred horses; the barn was by far the largest in the city.

The company was now using twenty-eight cars in regular service to handle the basic service. These included the original ten cars, the nineteen purchased in 1887 and several more acquired in 1890 and 1891. The cars no longer carried the company name painted on the side. Instead they appeared more like a billboard with the route name and streets served painted on the

One of the newest horse cars, #33 built about 1890, on Creighton Avenue. This was the "Belt Line" joining the two southerly lines and creating the only loop operation.

sides and ends. This system was inconvenient as it permanently attached a car to a particular route unless it was completely repainted. A later system produced a more practical and flexible four-sided destination sign. All of these cars carried a two-man operating crew, a driver and a conductor; the wages were low but the nickels continued to pour in.

Calhoun Street was suffering traffic congestion, so additional trackage was laid on Clinton Street from Main to Lewis, connected to Calhoun at Lewis, and extended east to Walton Avenue. This brought the Lewis Street line into being in 1890 without creating further clutter on Calhoun Street.

The Jenny Electric Works had now become the Fort Wayne Electric Works and many people were very interested in the new electric marvels that were being produced there. Hardly a week would go by without Mr. McDonald's works turning out something new to the public. The associated Jenny Electric Light and Power Company, in 1883 was busy building a new generating station on Spy Run Avenue at Kamm Street. This was a steam station and a successor to an earlier venture which had planned to use the Wabash and Erie Canal's feeder canal and reservoir to turn a turbine type generator. This had been a miserable failure and the new company got its water supply from the St. Joseph River across the street.

The large stables at the East Barns became a total loss in a fire that swept the building on December 23, 1890. The fire department responded swiftly to the call but the highly combustible straw and hay gave the fire too much of a head start. The building exploded in to flames so quickly that sixty horses perished in the holocaust before help arrived. The adjoining car barns were damaged but saved from being lost. The barns were rebuilt and a new but smaller stable replaced the old one.

Marmaduke M. M. Slattery of the electric works made a number of battery-power, propulsion experiments on bicycles and wagons and eventually got to the horse car situation. Mr. Slattery was one of many inventors throughout the country trying to improve street railway operations with electric power. Some used overhead wires, while others tried an underground conduit, but Slattery preferred storage batteries and he fitted out a horsecar with twenty-five eight-pound batteries and one motor. Later on the night of November 11, 1891, to avoid startling any horses, this car was loaded with forty-six people. It made a trip on the Belt Line reaching speeds up to 12 miles per hour![5] The car was rebuilt with a second motor but was unreliable and the unimpressed street railway decided to stick to horses. Mr. Slattery, a young man with a brilliant mind, was stricken ill and died shortly afterwards.

An untouched area known as the "Old Orchard" was acquired by a real estate firm and named "Lakeside". This area, immediately north of the Maumee and east of the St. Joseph River, was low and subject to flooding. This problem was partly solved with flood dikes and the digging of small ponds to collect run-off waters. These ponds were called lakes, with Delta Lake the largest, and provided nice park grounds. As early as 1890 a carline was contemplated for the area but little was done until 1892. The Lakeside Street Railroad Company was formed in August with a capital of $50,000.

The new company was fostered by Mr. McDonald, who owned $49,900 of the authorized stock. He planned to build east from Calhoun on Columbia Street, cross the river and terminate at Delta Lake![6] The company immediately met organized opposition which, more than likely, was quietly fostered by Fort Wayne Street Railroad. They no doubt felt that two companies were enough and three a crowd. Such points, as where the tracks would be laid on Columbia Street, the opposition to any tracks at all, and finally, a dispute over the propulsion of the cars plagued the new company. In a silent compromise the opposition ceased and the line was completed in late 1892 and, although a separate company, it was operated by Fort Wayne Street Railroad personnel and apparantly used their equipment. The other independent line, the Centlivre Company, extended its trackage by building east on the Hicksville Road, now East State, to Crescent Avenue and the newly established Driving Park.[17] (FOREST PK. BLVD.)

15

Nothing like a trolley outing, especially with car #13, a nice summer day, the Lewis Street Line and Fort Wayne Electric Railway — all for 5¢.

The lone seven bench open car turning north on to Calhoun Street. The decorations and crowd are for the 1895 Centenial celebration.

CHAPTER 2

The Magic of Electricity

Horses won the first bout with electricity but the management continued to think a better motive power might be available. The trade journals were full of stories of successful electrifications in city after city, and the cost savings that could be achieved without two sets of horses, their feed, care and housing. Electric street cars worked all day without complaint, they were thoroughly proven, and much needed in Fort Wayne.

With no fanfare, and in a series of rapid moves, the Fort Wayne Street Railway surprised the city with the magic of electricity. In March of 1892, they simply announced plans to spend $100,000 to electrify the system. The first move would be a power house at Clinton and Chestnut Streets ajoining the South Barns, and the second step, a fleet of new street cars. Rapid progress was made with three new electric street cars arriving in June. These were unloaded from the Nickel Plate spur track near the East Barns and towed to their new home in the remodeled barns. Representatives of the press were dispatched to cover this activity and they were soon able to report that more were arriving each day from the J. M. Jones Company of Watervliet, New York. These stories of more than thirty new cars created much curiosity and speculation.[1] At the same time a steady procession of new poles and miles of copper wire arrived to be erected at a fast pace.

The company manager, Mr. M. Stanley Robison, ran one of the new open electric cars over the West Main — East Washington line on July 8, 1892. Initial power came from Jenny Electric Light and Power as the new Chestnut Street Station was not completed. Work progressed so well that on August 28th the last horsecars, except Centlivre's, were withdrawn as the trolley bell clanged in the electric car era and sounded the death knell for the horsecars.

The new powerhouse went into service just in time to save the Jenny plant from over strain. The large flywheel of the Corliss engine was a great attraction to youngsters who watched the big reciprocating steam engine drive the generators. The horsecars were no longer needed and the best ones were sold with the rest junked, disappearing as did the old title. The company was sold for one dollar to the Fort Wayne Electric Railway to proudly proclaim the new era. In the interests of better service the old Bloomingdale line on Cass Street was replaced with a new double track line on Wells and extended north to Huffman Street.

The new firm was capitalized at $1,000,000 par value of stock. Most of this stock stayed in Fort Wayne hands. The electrification costs were met in a mortgage to the Guaranty and Indemnity Company of New York. This was for an issue of $600,000 in bonds all of which were issued.[2]

The life of the employee was not always the easiest, but it must have held some glamour as the old timers love to spin "street caring tales." The motorman and conductor were subjected to all types of weather, which, in itself, might not have been so bad, but often other duties remained for the crews after the little cars rolled back to the barn. No one was overpaid and the clamor over wages was climaxed by a strike of motormen and conductors from May 29 to June 3, 1893. They demanded a ten per cent increase from thirteen and one-half cents an hour to a flat fifteen cents and a company statement that twelve hours constituted a working day. The company refused to negotiate and tried to continue service but the strikers resisted, did some damage and threatened to do more. The labor movement sympathizers were then threatened by the city law enforcement. Before things got too bad, the company relented and granted the employees' request.[3]

The Centlivre brewery company was no longer interested in retaining the street railway operation particularly in view of the impending necessity to electrify. As a result the Centlivre line was sold to the Fort Wayne Electic Railway June 27, 1894 for $18,000. No service changes were made and the horsecars continued to run while the new owners sought franchise agreements from the city and county to electrify and extend the line.[4] The permission was granted and the line was electrified to the brewery by July 4 allowing swift service to the beer garden. On August 9 the remaining, former Centlivre, horse cars were called in as electric horsepower replaced the last hay burners in Fort Wayne.

"It is the proud boast of Fort Wayne, that while in almost every city of the United States, including all the greater ones, horses and mules are still used to propel street cars on some lines." This opening statement appeared under the heading of "Our Superb Electric Railway System" in the twentieth anniversary special issue of the FORT WAYNE NEWS, and gave a rather flamboyant description of the line in 1894.

"There are twenty miles of track in the system of the Fort Wayne Electric railway company. It has fifty-seven new and commodious coaches, of the latest and most luxurious pattern known to manufactures of street railway carriages, and twelve trailers. Mammoth sprinklers keep the track free from dust in the summer, and huge cyclone snow plows quickly remove the winter's snow. The introduction of electricity as a means of propelling street cars in the city of Fort Wayne has solved the problem of rapid transit for our people. The cars are run as rapidly as is consistent with the safety of people using the streets for the purposes for which they are intended, and passengers have no cause to complain of delays or loss of time in passing from one part of the city to another.

The plant at which power is generated for the street railway system is a model in every respect. Located near the center of the system, it furnishes easily abundant power to transact all that is required of it, not only to meet every day demands but also to supply any exigencies that can possibly arise out of any unusual influx of visitors, or the necessity of carrying large numbers of our own citizens on any special occasion. The three huge engines, of two hundred and seventy-five horse power each, that drive the dynamos to generate electricty for the large system are the product of the great Bass Foundry of this city, and the dynamos are made by the Thomson-Houston Company, of which the Fort Wayne Electric Company is an important and rapidly expanding branch."[5]

The arrival of the electric street car brought still another revolution to the city. Nearly half of the new fleet were eight-bench open summer cars which were designed for utility but soon proved to be very attractive to a pleasure seeking public. The open trolleys were a tremendous success and, in those days before the wheezing of the first auto had been heard, the trolley had many virtues of luxury and elegance. For a few cents anyone could ride through every section of town, enjoying the gentle sway and the breeze generated by the car's movement. Consequently an exciting new fad developed — the "Street Car Party." Trolleys became interesting and glamorous when an evening dinner party was climaxed with a ride through the city on a special car — and at a cost which all could afford. The company was only too happy to oblige and the following comments from the newspaper show how popular the fad became. On July 9 ten street car parties were held, on July 21 mention was made of fifty-three such parties in the past week and in August it was noted that "trolley parties have become the rage and half a score such parties take place each evening making a tour of all the city lines." One can easily imagine the laughter and gaiety radiating from an open trolley filled with young people. Truly the company had a new and unexpected source of revenue. The public was in love with the trolleys.

The citizens may have been happy and content but the employees were not. In 1894, the management attempted to cut the wages to twelve and one-half cents an hour but finally dropped the idea. In 1895 the attempt was again made, in earnest, and the car men walked out. Service was maintained with Pinkerton detectives riding the cars. The Trade and Labor Council ordered all union members to boycott the cars. Public opinion was on the worker's side and again the company backed down, but won one point in not re-hiring some discharged employees.

Several "phantom" trolley companies appeared in the early 1890's and in the next decade and a half over a dozen of these paper traction lines appeared. Some actually did a little preliminary grading and bridge work but perished in the early planning stages. Most of these were legitimate efforts begun by people who had little idea of finance and costs. One of these was concocted by C. E. Everett who started work on a line to Columbia City. This venture was harmless enough but he also proposed a ridiculous scheme to replace the Fort Wayne Electric Railway with a new company if the city would grant him an exclusive franchise. The whole idea was rejected and his complete undertaking fell in. A line to Hicksville, Ohio was also started but ran out of money.[6]

On November 11, 1895 articles of incorporation were filed for the Fort Wayne Consolidated Railway Company. Capitalization was doubled to $2,000,000. Fort Wayne Electric Railway was purchased December 4, 1895 for a consideration of one dollar. The sale conveyed all rights, franchises, properties and debts to the new firm. For all practical purposes the old company ceased to exist.[7]

At this time the company had seven routes; No. 1 Belt Line; No. 2 Bloomingdale, Hanna Street and Walton Avenue Line; No. 3 Main Street Line; No. 4 Jefferson Street Line; No. 5 Spy Run Avenue Line; No. 6 Race Track Line, and No. 7 Lewis Street Line.

One of the reasons for this increase was to keep the vogue of trolley pleasure riding growing. The new firm felt that an excellent traffic generator would be an amusement park of large proportions. Everything would have to be in the best of taste and designed to attract all ages, groups and interests, and the desired location was available.

Fort Wayne Electric Works on Broadway decorated for the Centenial. A single truck car, with one vestibule closed, stopped for the Pennsylvania R.R. crossing. Some of these buildings still stand inside the present Broadway works of General Electric.

Brand new line and brand new cars in June 1896. Cars 91 and 121 carrying "Swift Park Line" signs are on the partly ballasted tracks. This right-of-way is between the St. Joseph River and the Feeder Canal.

CHAPTER 3

Splendid Robison Park

The Wabash and Erie Canal was the longest man made canal in the world, but the completed canal operated as a unit for only a brief period. The upper end, near Fort Wayne, was already falling into disuse as a result of the railroads, when the southern portion was completed. The highest elevation on the canal was reached at Fort Wayne with ascending locks in either direction. This peak point created the name "Summit City" which continues to persist.

The main canal westward from Fort Wayne to Huntington and eastward from Fort Wayne required a steady water supply with a sufficient head of pressure for the locks. To accomplish this, the canal builders had erected, in 1834, a dam seven miles northeast of Fort Wayne and just below a large horseshoe bend in the St. Joseph River. The impounded water was conveyed to the main canal by means of a feeder canal with a storage reservoir in Fort Wayne just south of the present State and east of Clinton streets.[1] The big feeder dam was constructed of heavy timbers and debris and anchored to stone filled cribs. A guard lock kept the water level consistent. The deep water provided a pretty lagoon and swelled the river for several

The Main Pavilion overlooked the landing dock for the popular steam launch "Clementina". This 1896 setting shows the lagoon full of water.

Boating facilities at Robison were very popular. The naptha launch (above) later blew-up. The main docking area, near the band stand is shown below. Rowboats could be rented from this early "marina". The naptha launch and the steamboat Clementina are at the left in this 1896 scene.

Car 119 loading a crowd at the Robison Park terminal late in a summer afternoon. The Main Pavilion is at the right. One of the Park policemen can be seen, leaning on a cane.

miles. The west side had high bluffs and groves of trees. The dam, still in existance, was in need of repair by 1896 as was the feeder canal.

The management of the Consolidated Company purchased 265 acres of the adjacent land, acquired the rights to the dam and canal, and announced a $300,000 developement program in late 1895. On December 27, contracts were let for a seven mile double track line, using the feeder canal banks, and twenty-five new open cars. Promotions for Swift Park, with a picture of the main pavilion on the back of all tickets, began as part of a continuous and active publicity program. Work commenced immediately on a feverish basis to try to complete the job by the next June.

The new rail line was a 4.83 mile extension starting from the canal bridge on Spy Run north on Clinton, then the Fort Wayne-Leo Road, to Centlivre Park. From that point the line ran down the hill to the feeder canal and then on to the park site.[2] The line was built as quickly as possible and materials were hauled to the park to construct the new buildings. On May 30, 1896 the first open car ran to the park and back with city and company officials. The park was informally opened on June 13 to the interested and curious, but much work remained to be done. In deference to many requests from the citizens the company changed the name of Swift Park to Robison Park in honor of the General Manager M. Stanley Robison.

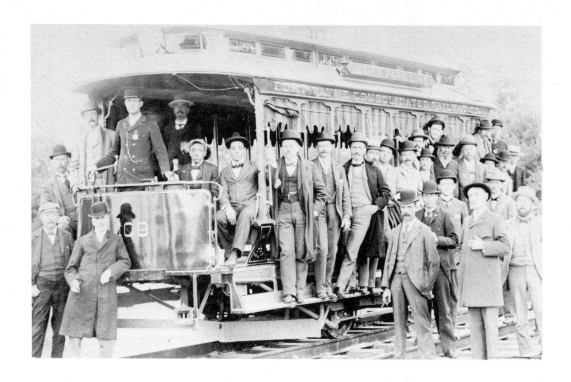

Two of the typical crowds visiting the park. The group (above) was one of the earliest as the car carries a Swift Park sign. Eight cars (below), in a typical weekend line-up, load a convention group. For years people came from far and near for a day at the park.

A spectacular Grand Opening was held on July 4 when over 35,000 people went out on the cars, a supreme test of the hauling capacity of the line. Cars rolled on a two minute headway hauling two and three open trailers. Many special features, acts and attractions were included on this first big day to set the pace for years to come.

The management wanted a high calibre operation and allowed no intoxicants sold on the premises. They hired their own police force to enforce the regulations and also saw to it that the primary entrance to the park could only be made by trolley. For those who felt the need of a glass of beer, the cars stopped halfway up the river at the suspension footbridge where thirsty travelers could cross the river to Germania Park - not a street railway venture.

The principal building was the big, main pavilion with four circular corner towers. This building was the center of park activities and usually flag bedecked to represent the various clubs that visited the park. It contained a cafe, dancing and party facilities and a huge electrically operated organ or Orchestron. This instrument could produce the general effect of a large and complete orchestra with sufficient volume to be heard in almost every area of the park. Water was supplied from a high stone water tower designed to represent a dutch windmill. Below the pavilion were the docks and boathouses. Several naptha launches, about one hundred row boats and a steamboat, the Clementina, operated from here. This continued until 1905 when the badly deteriorated dam was almost completely washed away returning the river to its original level, restricting water activities to canoes and small boats.

Another dance hall was built near the center of the park where the car line looped around a large grass and flower plotted area before a trim depot and waiting room. Spare tracks provided car storage for the heavy traffic. A theatre seating about nine hundred people was a popular attraction and found Robison Park on the routine vaudeville circuit.

A rustic bridge connected this area to the amusement area beyond a small bay. In the bay, on an island, was the tall steel-towered circle swing. Just over the way, on the high ground was a large roller coaster. Many lesser concessions and refreshment stands were in the roller coster area and extended to the shoot-the-chutes which gave pleasure seekers a sixty-foot drop, one hundred and fifty-foot mad-dash to the water.[3]

The park had its own agents to attract crowds and they arranged excursions from all over the area to bring crowds of people to the park. Some trips came from as far as Detroit and Indianapolis and often in conjunction with the steam railroads.

At all times Robison Park presented a well groomed appearance, with beautiful lawns, gardens, and well-trimmed sidewalks. The big buildings as well as all the lesser structures, such as bandstands, always appeared freshly painted. The rustic touch was carefully preserved yet neat and tidy. Excellent grounds maintainence was always the objective of the large ground crews. All of these things made a day's outing a joyful and relaxing experience, which was not soon forgotten as evidenced by the hundreds of people that still hold fond remembrances of the park. Many romances developed from an outing followed by the breezy ride home on the open car swaying down the moonlit river valley.

The Consolidated company was paying for these major improvements with more borrowed money. This time a mortgage was executed to the Guardian Trust Company of Cleveland for $1,500,000 in bonds. The ink was barely dry on the bonds when Frank DeH. Robinson had a falling out with his fellow owners. He took the company to court and placed it in receivership, September 1896. M. S. Robison and J. H. Bass were declared co-receivers. Robison resigned and Howell C. Rockwell replaced him. The receivership bounced around the court for three years in mass confusion.

Fort Wayne Electric Railway came back to life in the claims filed by the Guaranty and Indemnity Company. Receivers were demanded for the sold company and its bonds a first lien on the Consolidated company. These bonds were in default as were the Consolidated company's own bonds. The Cleveland firm made a rapid appearance also claiming first lien. Everybody came forward in a rush demanding their money.

The court had its hands full and finally handed down a lengthy decision on July 14, 1899. Everyone holding property belonging to the Consolidated company was ordered to return it. Robinson held certain properties and Bass held the twenty-five new open cars. In the same decree the company was ordered sold to satisfy all claims. Actually both companies had to be sold and the Fort Wayne Electric Railway finally terminated. The company was sold to George H. Garretson of Cleveland. The Fort Wayne Traction Company was organized on October 26, 1899 and the property was transferred, for $1,092,000, to the new company on November 8, 1899.[4] In the purchase local ownership disappeared for nearly fifty years.

R. T. McDonald died on Christmas Eve 1898 ending a most brilliant and spectacular career in finance and the electrical industry. It was through McDonald's efforts that the Fort Wayne Electric Works was still in the city. After it was sold to the Thomson - Houston Company the new owners wanted to move the pioneering firm east. It stayed in Fort Wayne becoming the nucleus of the big General Electric complex.

The Lakeside Street Railway, as part of McDonald's estate became a court problem. The line's dollar value was quite low and the estate refused to spend any money on it. The City Council ordered the Consolidated company to re-lay the tracks in accordance with a paving program. The Consolidated company, also in the courts, refused, maintaining they only operated the line and not supposed to maintain it. By July 12, 1900 the Knickerbocker Trust Company of New York sued to collect on the bonds which were now in default. Albert L. Scott, the receiver, was ordered to sell the company to the highest bidder. Fort Wayne Traction Company offered $25,000 for the company and bought it on December 31.[5] This action unified all the street realway operations and a status quo was expected. An entirely new phase was about to begin for Fort Wayne and its traction company. A whole quiet way of life was about to change, but no one realized it.

Cars 111 and 127, two of the new, nine - bench opens on the line in June, 1896. The route, as can be seen, was anything but straight. The Feeder Canal builders followed a water level route which was full of tight curves.

CHAPTER 4

Wabash Valley Interurban Empire

At the turn of the century, the wonderful world of electric railways became aware of intercity rail possibilities, above and beyond suburban operations. Many small towns and hamlets were already served by steam railroads while others had no rail facilities at all. As the lines reached out from town to town the new word "interurban" came into general use to describe the mushrooming electric railways. Indiana quickly became a center of activity. However, Fort Wayne, though quick to acquire a street railway, lagged on interurban development. The apathy probably arose from the traction company's ownership being transferred out of the city.

Numerous paper companies made little impression on the citizens, especially when nothing came of them. The incorporation of the Fort Wayne and Southwestern Traction Company seemed to be just another in the series. This company sounded a little more realistic and determined. The capitalization was announced as $600,000 and the acquisition of the abandoned Wabash and Erie Canal, from Fort Wayne to Huntington seemed promising. One of the quiet promotors of this venture was William B. McKinley who was building an empire of electric lines in Illinois.

The Southwestern line called itself the "Canal Route" using the ideal, but meandering, banks for its roadbed. Huntington landed the offices, shops and powerhouse by providing a cash subsidy. The line entered Fort Wayne over its own tracks via Taylor Street to Fairfield Avenue then north, jogging to Fulton Street, then east on Pearl Street to Harrison Street. The terminal was located at this latter intersection.[1]

A steam engine pulled a carload of Fort Wayne businessmen over the new route on September 30, 1901. By December 12 the first electric car made a trip from Fort Wayne to Huntington. Five wooden interurban cars were placed in service and the interurban boom had begun. After this first line had rolled into reality, the way was paved with golden prospects for the interurban promoters. Everybody became charged with enthusiasm except the somewhat alarmed railroads.

Loud noises were heard from Lima, Ohio with the proposal to build an interurban line to

Fort Wayne & Southwestern Railways #304, before it was placed on its trucks, on the transfer table at the John Stephenson Car Co.

Car #205 at the Wabash interurban station. This is the only known car lettered with the lenghty Fort Wayne, Logansport, Lafayette & Lima Traction Co. title, dating the picture as late 1904.

Fort Wayne. Work on the Fort Wayne, Van Wert, and Lima Traction Company began but a number of problems arose and the work was spasmodic in an off again - on again manner.

On March 24, 1903 notice was given that Fort Wayne Traction had been purchased by what was described as the Murdock Syndicate for $1,513,000 indicating an increase in value of $500,000 in four years. The exact nature of some of the improvements might have been questioned when a street car was derailed at Hoagland and Creighton Avenues because the car tracks sank out of sight in a sea of mud.

The year 1903 saw the new Southwestern line which now had a 45 mile line with an extension to Wabash, go into receivership and the first work done on the Fort Wayne - Springfield line. Far down the Wabash Valley, the Lafayette Street Railway was quietly taken over, on May 29 by a pretentious and formidable sounding company known as the Fort Wayne, Logansport, Lafayette, and Lima Traction Company. This was no mere promotional scheme based on hot air as this company had cash and sound backing. Presently it was to throw its weight the full length of the valley.[2]

This new organization changed its name to the Fort Wayne and Wabash Valley Traction Company, February 25, 1904 and quietly, but quickly, snatched up every line proposed or existing from Lafayette to Fort Wayne. The Fort Wayne and Wabash Valley title was to be one of the most descriptive names to appear through the corporate history. It was one of the notable "syndicate" formations designed to acquire large traction empires. This was Schoepf - McGowan Syndicate, which had acquired the local Fort Wayne lines. Among the prominent midwest and eastern traction personalities included in the syndicate were James, Charles, and Samuel

Wabash Valley #501, "Kenilworth" (above) as delivered by Cincinnati Car Co. in 1906. Sister car #503 (below), in 1923 and just before rebuilding, still shows its original exterior appearance.

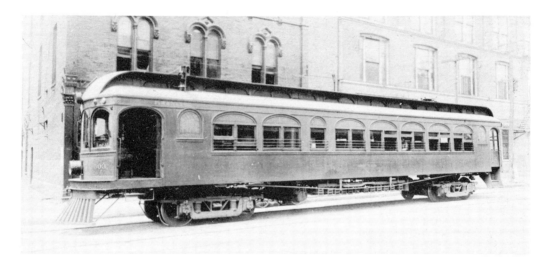

Murdock; J. Levering Jones and Hugh McGowan. McGowan of Indianapolis and W. Kesley Schoepf head of the Cincinnati St. Ry. were the representative heads of this strong syndicate. McGowan was the Indiana power while Schoepf ran things in Ohio, notably the putting together of the Ohio Electric System.[3] On February 27, 1904 they formally took over five companies; Fort Wayne Traction Co., Wabash River Traction Co., Wabash - Logansport Traction Co., Logansport Railway Co., and Logansport, Rochester and Northern Traction Co., The Fort Wayne and Southwestern was soon added to this group.[4]

Not all of these properties were in operation, or completed, at the time of the amalgamation. The Wabash River Traction Company was formed in 1900. It operated the Wabash City lines and the interurban from Wabash to Peru through a pleasant riverside grove known as Boyd Park. The Logansport Street Railway had been founded in 1882 and operated the street railway in that city. The Logansport, Rochester and Northern was mainly a promotion idea which built only a short stretch of track in Logansport. This trackage was turned over to the city lines and nothing further was built. The link between Peru and Logansport was completed by the Wabash Valley Lines for the Wabash - Logansport Traction Company. The syndicate also paid $25,000 for a right of way from Huntington to Marion but never built the line. On September 1, 1904 the first through Fort Wayne - Logansport run was made. This line roughly paralleled the Wabash Railroad which met the interurban's lower fares and engaged in a rate war to keep their passengers.

The Fort Wayne Electric Light and Power Company came into existence in July 1902. This was largely an outside group of investors who planned to build, own and operate a power and light

The passenger station and substation at Lagro were typical structures along the Wabash Valley route.

The 303, as originally built, at the Peru passenger terminal. It was considerably altered after the Kingsland accident.

system. On March 24, 1904 they bought the Jenny Electric Light and Power Company in a one dollar merger. This sort of transaction continued as the merged firm went to the Southwestern company on October 27, 1904, and the next day to the Wabash Valley Company. Both were one dollar transactions. Throughout these legal manuevers the power company retained its identity.[5] By early 1905 the power and traction company were the same. A huge, million dollar power station was planned near the existing Kamm Street plant on Spy Run Avenue.

Indiana Union Traction Company, one of the midwest traction giants, had a subsidiary line which, by now, reached Bluffton; and to keep them from building further, the Fort Wayne, Bluffton and Marion Traction Company was incorporated, April 25, 1905 to close the remaining distance to Fort Wayne. A hot and absurd race commenced for this stretch of track. The Fort Wayne crews building south crossed what is now Highway 1 south of Kingsland. As this construction gang raced south on the east side of the road they met the rival company's gang building north on the west side of the road four miles north of Bluffton. Both sides were prepared to build past the other before a truce was declared. The right of way north from Bluffton was turned over to the south bound company and the tracks again crossed the road to the meeting point. Until the last interurban car was run, these two unnecessary and treacherous grade crossings existed.

The Fort Wayne, Bluffton and Marion stock was owned by the Schoepf-McGowan interests and the company was officially deeded to the Wabash Valley on December 30, 1905.[6] These underlying companies were a handy way to raise new capital, through large bond issues, without upsetting the financial structure of the parent company. Full operation of the Bluffton line commenced on March 1, 1906 with cars entering Fort Wayne over the Broadway line.

A major rail gap remained unfilled which left the Lafayette lines separated. This was remedied by the formation of the Lafayette - Logansport Traction Company in 1906. Again the Fort Wayne and Wabash Valley owned all the stock and deeded the new line to themselves upon completion. This expensive extension was a grave error, touching only four small intermediate towns, including costly bridges, and often only a few yards from the Wabash Railroad. It so closely paralleled the Wabash that, at some points, it had the appearance of a secondary main line track. Even so, the company now had a 114 mile line stretching from Fort Wayne to Lafayette.

With all the new track extensions, new cars became imperative. The acquired pieces of rolling stock were small, slow and not befitting the mighty firm they represented. In May, 1906, plans were made for through Indianapolis - Fort Wayne trains via both Peru and Bluffton as a joint operation between the Wabash Valley System and the Union Traction lines. It was to be a "pool" service with each side putting cars in use. For their lines, the Wabash Valley acquired eleven, big, handsome interurban cars from the syndicate affiliate Cincinnati Car Company. Four of these were strictly deluxe, "limited" Observation - Buffet cars for the "Wabash Valley Flyer" operation using the Fort Wayne - Indianapolis route via Peru. Equally fine were the Union Traction cars for the "Hoosierland" operation corresponding service via Bluffton. In all the history of electric traction, marked by constant squabbles, there would not be another such successful service on two routes, each over 100 miles long, serving the public for over thirty years.[7] Union Traction's cars also swung from their curved Wabash River bridge to the Wabash Valley's tracks to enter Logansport.

During this period of rapid expansion by the Fort Wayne and Wabash Valley, three other interurban companies made their entrances into Fort Wayne over local car lines. These were also built by other outside interests. In late 1905, the Fort Wayne, Van Wert and Lima Tranction Company after many false starts finally entered the city from the east. Regular service to New Haven began on September 19. The "Lima" line, open September 19, provided an important connecting link between the traction systems of northern Indiana and Ohio, for both the passenger and the increasing less than carload (l. c. l.) freight business. The same company effectively siphoned the local passenger trade held by the Pittsburg, Fort Wayne & Chicago lines

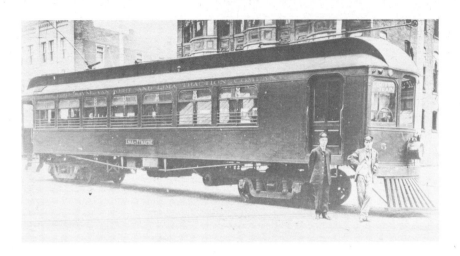

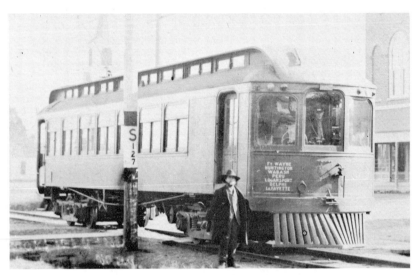

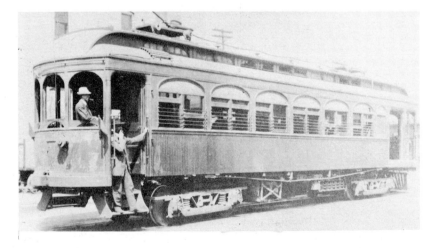

Top: Fort Wayne, Van Wert & Lima Traction Co. #5, in 1905. Middle: Wabash Valley #302 at the Rockfield Station. Bottom: Fort Wayne & Springfield Ry. Co. car as equipped for A.C. operation at the Fort Wayne terminal. The car is 1, 2 or 3.

of the Pennsylvania Railroad. This new line was leased to the Lima - Toledo Traction Company in 1906, and, in 1907, fell into the hands of W. K. Schoepf's giant Ohio Electric Railway consolidated group. The Lima line was destined to be nothing more than a pawn during the rest of its career.

To the north, a much ballyhooed line known as the Toledo and Chicago Interurban Railway Company was looking over the sparse possibilities of northeastern Indiana. The prospects looked quite slim and the promoters, wanting something tangible for the stockholders, elected to build the "Fort Wayne Division". This was the first A. C., Single Phase, powered line to enter the city. Car number one made the first trip on "May Day," 1906 with regular service beginning on May tenth. The tracks extended north to Garrett, then meandered in two directions to Waterloo and Kendallville. This huge half circle of trackage anchored at Garrett provided an interesting operation and scheduling problem for the duration of the line's existence. After struggling to take passengers from both the Grand Rapids & Indiana (Pennsylvania owned) and the Fort Wayne, Jackson and Saginaw (N.Y.C. lines), unsuccessfully, the firm fell into receivership in February 1908.

The Fort Wayne and Springfield Railway Company continued a slow struggling battle to build from Fort Wayne to Decatur. Financial backing was slow to appear and the line was built in bits. Farmers along the way contributed material and labor in return for promises of convenient transporation for themselves and their produce. The company initially ordered cars in 1904 but had to postpone the order. By the summer of 1905 the grading was nearly complete but no tracks were laid. Finally at the late date of February 1, 1907 the first service commenced. The company located its office, shop and power house at Decatur still anticipating building on to Springfield. The firm had been ambitiously planned and was another experimental application of alternating current. The use of A.C. was hoped to reduce operating costs but the reverse happened. Due to a consistent lack of capital and business the line was never greatly improved nor extended to Springfield. This was a prime example of an interurban line that should never have been built.

Most traction lines were powered by Direct Current of varying voltage, usually 600 volts. D.C. motors presented fewer problems and were better suited to street railway operation. Most interurbans stemming from street car lines used the same D.C. voltage. The use of Alternating Current applications was in its infancy and presented many new problems. Oddly enough, Fort Wayne had two of the few A.C. lines built, and each had a different voltage. The Toledo and Chicago used 3,300 volts while the Fort Wayne - Springfield used 6,600.[8]

Another directly related line was the Marion, Bluffton & Eastern Traction Company, which literally threw down thirty-seven miles of track between Marion and Bluffton. It opened for service on December 15, 1906, locating its offices at Bluffton. Ridiculous, though it may appear, the financially weak company controlled the still weaker Bluffton, Geneva and Celina Traction Company through Mr. L. C. Justus who envisioned a connection with the Western Ohio Railway. This latter company ran a single car up and down an eighteen-mile stretch, from Bluffton to Geneva, of the never completed line.

These were the great days for the interurbans. The cars had a majestic glamour and magic appeal to young and old alike. Cars of five distinct companies were in constant attendance at the Fort Wayne Terminal. Long and racy or short and stubby wooden cars, well maintained with gilt lettering and trim, made an impressive array. Limiteds and locals nosed slowly onto Main Street shoving the few automobiles out of the way with complete disdain. The big cars trundled their way docily to the city limits. From there on it was all power and full speed as the interurbans counted on making their best time when on their own private tracks. Few will forget the loud toot of the whistle and the flurry of dust, as another country grade crossing was left behind. The big cars of the Wabash Valley, Union Traction and Ohio Electric always excited the imagination.

A three way meet at Garrett on the Toledo & Chicago Interurban Railway Company lines. The car to the right is headed for Waterloo, the one in the center to Kendallville and the one on the left to Fort Wayne. These two passenger cars and the express motor are pictured about 1910.

T. & C. #1 (left) entering the Kendallville yards. This may have been the first trip over the line. Typical resourcefulness (right) produced this T. & C. construction locomotive, hardly more than an off-center outhouse on a motorized flat car.

T. &. C. #51 pulling, borrowed and already out-of-date, Union Traction Company #237. This car was used during the 1906 construction period. Motor and trailer (below) are loading a large crowd at Garrett.

A whole way of life was changing and the midwest was growing in a new way. The city dwellers could travel easily, quickly and conveniently from the home town and do it at low cost. Small rural communities, largely dependent on themselves for years, now found the cities close at hand. Farm produce was easily moved and the people with it. Autos and good roads were still in the future but people were beginning to move. Trips that took a whole day or several days were reduced to hours or one day. It was no wonder that everyone took to the interurban railway. Unfortunately it would also be its great undoing, but no one could see ahead. However, Henry Ford and the Model T were just around the corner.

Often the "Lawton", the Wabash Valley's private car, could be seen pompously hauling the company dignitaries or scooting about on a chartered excursion. Union Traction's "Martha" might be in town too, if President Arthur W. Brady chose to go visiting.

Various buildings were needed for the several companies. Each firm had to have a carbarn and, unless they bought their electricity, a power house. Some of these facilities were used for years but the small power stations were uneconomical and were closed as fast as the line was consolidated with the big company.

The Logansport property consisted of two substantial, concrete steel and brick buildings housing the station, offices and shops. The outside ends were closed and access to the three tracks was made by a transfer table located in the middle. The design was a miniature of a large city barn design for use in congested areas, although the Logansport location was anything but crowded. One pit-track allowed light repairs to city cars.

The Huntington plant was the best equipped with the shop and powerhouse located between First Street and the Erie Railroad. The Powerhouse was closed in 1907 but retained for storage

The Spy Run Avenue power house upon completion in 1907. The building, of a new design and arrangement, was soon rivaled by the municipal City Light plant.

The Huntington power house (above) was closed after 1907. A wooden 300 series cars is on the yard storage track. (Below) Home base for the Southwestern line, the Huntington Shops handled all interurban rebuilding and maintainance.

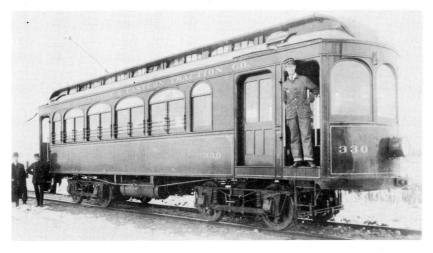

Marion, Bluffton & Eastern Traction Co. #330 as delivered and new. The very light trackwork and the missing car pilot show the hasty construction.

Two views of the Kendallville power house. (Above) The east side shows the yard and car #1. To the right is the coaling dock which which is shown (below) in detail, with freight motor #50.

and the substation. The slate-roofed, brick shop covered an area of 13,680 feet with the lumber shed adjoining it. This shop had been built as the center point location, home-base for the South-western line. It was designed to handle all major repairs and consequently had four pit-tracks and a complete machine shop. Interurban new construction, major rebuilds and heavy repairs continued there for many years.

Wabash River Traction constructed a large four-track barn and powerhouse between Wabash and Peru at a picnic area along the river called Boyd Park. It was a popular attraction but very isolated for operating purposes. After the consolidation the building was used for storage serving a practical use for many years.[9]

Along with Boyd Park, other parks had been acquired in both Lafayette and Logansport. Spencer Park, in east Logansport on the Eel River contained about eighteen acres of grounds used primarily for dances, picnics and ball games. Tecumseh Trail Park near Lafayette was smaller but quite popular. None of these small parks could be much more than a very poor second to the stellar attraction of Robison Park which would continue as Indiana's number one park. Locally, however, the parks would be kept as long as they remained traffic generators.

Kendallville, in anticipation of the building of a long east-west line was the main base for the Toledo and Chicago line. A large and handsome powerhouse was built to generate the 3300 volt A.C. current. Nearby stood the four-track brick and frame car barn. Repairs and rebuilding were done here until, in later years, it was found to be cheaper to have the work done by the Fort Wayne company.

The power situation was in control of the traction company. They were able to open the big Spy Run station on March 1. 1907 and this was to be the central generation point for the entire area. The station was a new design, attracting widespread engineering interest. Whole series of articles were printed in the leading engineering and traction journals. The old north power station and the city trolley line's Chestnut Street station were closed.

Mayor Hosey of Fort Wayne was much opposed to the traction company monopoly on electric power. He spearheaded a drive throughout 1906 to build a municipal power plant from funds originally levied as early in 1898. The question created a serious controversy and required a special election in November 1906 but the city generating station was begun in 1907. The City plant was opened in 1908 in direct competition to the Traction Company[10] Charges and counter-charges were hurtled back and forth between the traction company and the city for years. The gap between the two opposing views never closed and City Light continues today as a municipal power utility in competion with private power.

In 1910, the Fort Wayne and Wabash Valley came through with one of the typical, grandiose schemes conceived during this wide open period of interurban consolidations and expansions. The officials who ambitiously analyzed the company proposed the acquistion of the Fort Wayne & Springfield Railway Company; the Toledo & Chicago Interurban Railway; the Marion, Bluffton and Eastern Traction Company; and the Toledo and Indiana Traction Company. Three of these companies were in, or on the verge of serious financial difficulties.

The Toledo and Indiana had just came out of receivership and had a 56 mile line from the heart of Toledo to Bryan, Ohio. Bryan was but a scant 29 miles from a possible connection with the Toledo and Chicago Interurban Railway at Auburn, Indiana. Combined and joined, this would have provided a 225 mile, well built, through, trunk line interurban from Toledo, Ohio to Lafayette, Indiana.

Another extension was planned to Columbia City, nineteen miles along the Pennsylvania Railroad west of Fort Wayne. Franchises were secured for this line, and it was chartered as the Fort Wayne & Winona Traction Company. This title would indicate thoughts of reaching even further.

Such a large scale plan, if it were carried through, would have produced one of the largest and most powerful midwest interurban empires - and it almost did. All the preliminary negatiations were carried through, financing arranged, and, to make certain, careful studies were made of the entire cost of the extensions to the last tie and spike needed. Certain re-habilitations of the lines to be acquired were also figured and additional rolling stock estimates considered. Only the very weak Bluffton, Geneva & Celina Traction Company was omitted from this master plan as the little line was quite obiviously not worth the trouble.

The new organization and consolidation plan with its careful estimations was to be known as the Fort Wayne & Wabash Valley Traction and Terminal Company. This dream was kept under careful consideration awaiting the ''right'' moment and was finally presented in October, 1910.[11] By then the right moment had gone by and the dream was a nightmare.

Interurban lines often had mishaps involving several cars. Sometimes a big interurban would catch up with a small city car that made the mistake of stopping. Shop records show scattered reports of repairs to city cars munched or nipped by an interurban.Minor derailments were not uncommon. Occasionally the interurban cars themselves would meet head-on with a thundering smash that left twisted steel and heaps of kindling wood strewn about. Worse still was the possibility of the entire mess catching fire from an upset heater stove.

Car #307 of the Fort Wayne & Wabash Valley Traction Co. (above) after missing a curve and riding into a field, about 1912. Workers (below) prepare to rescue the wandering interurban car.

All to typical of M. B. & E. operation, with #330 in a 1913 accident near Warren. In the background is #325.

Catastrophe at Kingsland, September 21, 1910 - 303 through 233!

Such a smashing occurrence happened one-half mile north of the village of Kingsland on the Bluffton line, when on September 21,1910 Union Traction's #233 rolled northward with pleasure seekers bound for the Fort Wayne Fair. Southbound Wabash Valley #303, on that fateful day, running extra and empty with clear-cut meet orders, overran the specified meeting point and headed for another siding at full speed.

One individual was considering his lot most unfortunate. He had been left standing on the rear vestibule steps of #233 which was more than overloaded. The car was just beginning to pick up speed from the Erie R.R. crossing when, leaning back and peeking out, he caught a glimpse of the southbound car as it darted behind a grove of trees completely obscuring a long "S" curve. He jumped, landed safely, and seconds later in a resounding, earsplitting crash, the #233 had been overidden and telescoped more than half way by the higher, heavier car #303. Forty-one people, among them Mr. L. C. Justus, died in the crushed rubble. The #303 was salvaged and rebuilt, but the remains of the unfortunate #233 were burned on the spot by the wreck crews. The Kingsland disaster was the worst wreck in interurban history.

The accident had happened on the Wabash Valley's trackage. Their crew, though exonerated, was in the wrong, and a car had been totally destroyed. These were expensive items in terms of money, as well as prestige, but were insignificant when compared to the huge damage suits brought about by the death of forty-one persons and the injuries to many more.

The wreck at Kingsland, although the worst, was only one of several occuring in Indiana during this same period and brought on a detailed investigation by the Indiana Railroad Commission. The results were not favorable for the companies involved and produced strong criticism of the entire interurban industry. The Wabash Valley was cited for rather shoddy practices.

Investigations showed that southbound #303 was to clear all scheduled trains by five minutes. B. T. Corkwell, motorman, and Del Wilson, conductor, were two sidings beyond the ordered meeting point as they raced for siding 107 at Kingsland. Corkwell had been fired by the Union Traction Company and came to the Wabash Valley system to operate city streetcars. Somehow he was promoted to interurban service in April 1910 and proceeded to collect a considerable number of demerits for rule violations, including fifty for meeting a car at the wrong siding. Wilson, who nearly failed a written rules examination, was hired the day before the accident and probably did not appreciate the significance of the written orders.

The Wabash Valley's hiring standards and employee records were checked and it was found that Corkwell and Wilson were anything but exceptions to normal standards. Over an extended period, preceeding the accident, at least fifty motormen and conductors had either quit or been fired following serious rule infractions including, among others such as drunkedness, ignoring train orders, and the overrunning of meeting places. The Bluffton line, like most others, had no signaling system depending alone on competent carrying out of train orders. Later requirements demanded block signalling on the heavy traffic lines.[12]

The big company unexpectedly collapsed in the face of the catastrophe; it was completely unable to meet the ruinous claims of the "Kingsland Wreck." The firm was succeeded on February 25, 1911, by the Fort Wayne and Northern Indiana Traction Company. This new organization had enough inherited problems to cope with, and the great expansion plans were shelved and forgotten. The dream had been shattered in one split second, and the plans were quietly allowed to gather dust.

A Union Traction Co. steel 400 series cars nosing around the old canal bed at the Lagro, Wabash Valley - Wabash R. R., interlocking plant. The car had run through the protecting derail.

CHAPTER 5

The Lean Teens

The struggling Marion, Bluffton and Eastern soon went down. It was staggered by a nasty wreck near Marion on July 12, 1912. This had left the company financially embarrassed and came at the climax of a dispute with the construction firm that built the line. The owners and builders had feuded for some time over the poorly constructed trackwork which was ordered rebuilt by the Indiana Railroad Commission. Bankruptcy was the only answer with the firm emerging on July 1, 1914, as the Marion and Bluffton Traction Company. "Eastern" disappeared from the title as the new company tried to make a paying proposition of what it had.

The Bluffton, Geneva and Celina faced a more serious prospect. It had originally spurned the town of Berne in favor of Geneva when the latter's bank offered aid. As a planned connecting Indiana - Ohio link it would have run in the wrong direction, from Northwest to Southeast, when a Southwest to Northeast line such as the proposed Auburn - Bryan line was needed. When its major promoter, Mr. Justus, was killed the line was left in its short form with light passenger traffic and practically no freight business. In 1917 it was junked to aid the war effort.[1]

The two A.C. powered lines also underwent considerable change and received new titles that were more realistic. The Fort Wayne and Northwestern Railway Company succeeded the Toledo and Chicago when the line worked itself from beneath the receiver. In 1913, 600 volt direct current, the standard trolley voltage, replaced the older 3300 Alternating Current system. The

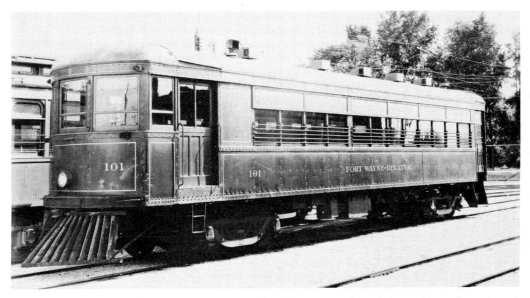

Fort Wayne - Decatur #101 at the Spy Run Shops in August 1928. The car was no longer being used in regular service and the wooden pilot was only a temporary addition as the car was delivered with an undermounted steel pilot.

Shop interior (above) of the old Chestnut Street power house with Union Traction 429 on the pit track. (Below) Part of the ugly collection of buildings on Baker Street.

Fort Wayne and Springfield collapsed in 1912 later emerging as the Fort Wayne and Decatur Traction Company in 1916. During the next year they disposed of the original 6600 volt, 25 cycle, single-phase system and the old cars. The new cars were equipped for 1200 volt D.C. operation and were rushed into service very quickly when the powerhouse burned destroying the old generating station. The Decatur line remained completely independent although it was in the same operating hands as the Fort Wayne and Northern Indiana.

During this heyday period of the interurbans changes and improvements continued on the Fort Wayne City Lines, through the purchase of new cars and extensions to the trolley lines. The car barn area on Chestnut Street was also expanded in piecemeal bits. West of the old power-house four metal sheds were erected for car repair and material storage. The westermost build-ing which was torn down and not replaced had four pit tracks. As a result much work had to be done in the out-of-doors, regardless of the weather. This must have presented the most adverse conditions, although one entire group of city cars were built at the South Barns and extensive rebuilding carried on. Unfortunately the whole conglomeration of buildings, at best, made a very poor appearance and must have given alighting Pennsylvania Railroad passengers a rat-her rude shock for their first impression of the city.

A six track car barn, with no doors, and the old stable building occupied the north side of the Baker Street complex.

The Broadway line was extended south to the Bluffton Bridge in 1903 as Fort Wayne Traction embarked on its improvement program. The same year the South Wayne line was created by laying rails south from Creighton to Organ Street, now Kinsmoor. South Calhoun was extended to Pontiac and east on Pontiac to Walton. The Lewis line was extended east to Wabash Avenue and Maumee. The Huffman line was made by extending the tracks west of Wells to Jessie Street.

As each interurban line arrived extensions were made to the street railway to provide proper entrance. New trackage was built west from Broadway on Taylor to give the Southwestern line an entrance and also provided a new city car line. The line to Bluffton merely hooked onto the end of the Broadway line as did the Toledo and Chicago by connecting to the city system near Wells and Sixth Streets. The Lewis line was again extended east on Maumee to Warren and south on Chestnut, a different Chestnut than where the barns were located, over private right-of-way. This provided an entrance for the Lima line. The Decatur line entered the city over South Calhoun Street.

During the era of the Fort Wayne and Northern Indiana many of the earlier street cars were showing their age and they presented an expensive maintenance problem. The "Pay-As-You-Enter" system was introduced and the "nearside" car adopted for the city lines, in 1913. Twenty-six new cars were purchased to meet the new operating plan. These single truck cars were quite long with most of the overhang in front. One group of cars from the J. G. Brill Company was not particularly successful because the extreme length produced a wobbling gait. With a large, front-platform load these cars literally kicked up their heels as the rear wheels lifted off the rails.

Little new trackage was built but numerous "wyes" were constructed at the end of most lines to turn the single end, nearside cars. The only major new work was an extension of the South Wayne line to one block south of Rudisill completed in 1916. The city trackwork was rapidly falling into disrepair and becoming incapable of carrying heavier traffic.[2]

Hard luck had dogged the heels of the Fort Wayne & Northern Indiana. Born in trouble, the

Home built 123 drifting along on a Spring day in 1905.

Spy Run Avenue was a sea of mud, insuring good street car patronage and little vehicle traffic, when Jones built 119 headed south from the new power plant in 1907.

One of the 120 series of city cars on West Creighton Avenue near Miner Street.

Nearside 218 running south on Calhoun in 1913 as an alighting passenger runs for the new Pennsylvania depot. The railroad elevation was new at this time.

company's life was plagued with tough luck stories. Part of the walls of the Boyd Park barn blew out in a tornado settling the heavy slate roof and supporting steel girders on top of a number of stored cars. The Spring floods of 1913 played havoc down the entire Wabash River Valley. All bridges, highway, railroad, interurban etc. were damaged or wrecked by the swirling waters. In Lafayette, the Main Street bridge was weakened and collapsed.[3] It carried the Lafayette City Lines, West Lafayette routes and the Battleground suburban line. Naturally the interurban company was assessed for the reconstruction of the link. One span of the big Wild Cat Creek bridge was washed away in a raging torrent. Many other bridges also needed repairs and strengthening. Extensive reconstruction of city trackage in Fort Wayne, Logansport and Lafayette would also be necessary in the next few years. These problems were capped by a prolonged strike and boycott throughout 1915, coupled with the rise of the jitney bus, which pushed revenues ever lower in Fort Wayne.

The Boyd Park barn (above) from the south side wye, showing the walls blown out in a tornado. Several cars were damaged or destroyed. The west side view (below) shows the rebuilt barn which was used for storage.

Ten, new, double truck cars arrived in 1917 to handle the heavy traffic lines. These cars were better riding than the small cars and the greater seating capacity meant that two new cars could carry the same number as three small cars. In an era of rising costs this meant one less two man crew, and the company was in financial trouble. Within a few months, after the arrival of the big cars, the company was met with loud demands from the bondholders to make good the outstanding debts.

Throughout 1918, another exhaustive analysis of the company was completed to study the reasons behind an apparent failure. The report presented this opinion: The capitalization was faulty to the point where a fair return could not be earned on portions of the line. The Lafayette - Logansport stretch, by now an obvious and unhappy construction blunder, and the Lafayette City Lines could probably be well dispensed with. Their high fixed charges were considered an unecessary burden on the Fort Wayne and Northern Indiana line. One happy suggestion was that both these links might be better run if they were dumped and turned over to the underlying bondholders (this group took a rather dim view of the idea). The system was over-tracked and the depreciation reserve account was excessively high.[4] Operating costs were also on a slow, steady increase.

Robert M. Feustel, the president, was named receiver on February 8, 1919. He continued the much needed equipment rehabilitation program, adding more than sixty new single-truck city cars of an advanced design. Conversion to one-man operation of some existing cars was commenced with the hope of further reducing costs. The property was sold at a foreclosure sale, December 29, 1919, to representatives of the Bondholders Protective Committee, although Feustel continued to operate the property until April 30, 1920.

During this corner-cutting period, Robison Park fell an untimely victim of economy. Unfortunately the park was served by a long rail line that ran profitable service for only four months of the year. Car service was provided year round with four daily trips, during the off season, made by a double truck closed car to buck the snow. Although the park continued to be a leading attraction people began coming by automobile and trolley riding dropped. Declining revenues were not enough to meet the continued costs of first class maintainance or meet the rehabilitation expense that would be coming in the near future, especially when the company went into receivership. There would also be no new open cars to replace the aging two-man cars. President Feustel issued a simple statement to the press that the park would not open for the 1920 season. This was the final word following a series of threats as the line lost money. The tracks were torn up back to Parnell Avenue, in the first retrenchment of the rail lines.

The tiny remainder from Spy Run and State to Parnell was called the Centlivre Short Line (#13). Later, the tracks on North Clinton were taken up and moved down to the canal bed so that the line curved onto its own right-of-way as it swung by the brewery. The line served the "Riverview" area but was not a money maker. It could continue to exist as long as the line needed no major maintenance.

Double trucker 254 on the Robison Park line. These cars were not frequently used in Fort Wayne service except during the winter months and then only on the Park line.

Brand new #240, first of the steel, two man cars delivered in 1917.

Line car and crew putting the finishing touches on the new span of the Wildcat Creek bridge.

CHAPTER 6

The Indiana Service Corporation

On January 15, 1920, a bright new star appeared on the horizon when the Indiana Service Corporation (I. S. C.) was incorporated. Within a few days the bondholders committee accepted a proposal to deliver the Fort Wayne and Northern Indiana Traction Company to the I. S. C. in a stock exchange. The Lafayette City Lines were avoided, and that system went to it's bond-holders. However, from March 1922 until abandonment March 13, 1923, I. S. C. was saddled with an isolated three mile stretch to Battleground. At the same time the Wabash Valley Utili-ties, another power company, was delivered to I. S. C. The new corporation officially assumed control May 1, 1920, with Feustel as president. With a clean slate, I. S. C. began to push a vigorous new program throughout the twenties.

Memories of the Wabash Valley's proposed program also came back. Two of the independent interurban lines were in rugged financial difficulties. The Fort Wayne and Northwestern Railway Company was picked up at a receivers sale September 30, 1924, and became the Northern Division of I. S. C. Following a careful re-habilitation, a new menace appeared in the form of one of the many, paved roads which the state of Indiana was building in the twenties. This high-way took away traffic and served as a prelude of what was slowly to follow, everywhere, as more people turned to automobiles. Another sick neighbor was the old Fort Wayne - Lima line, which had been through the hands of several companies and in receivership since the collapse of the Ohio Electric in 1921. The poor outfit had been pumped dry, and the equipment, the same age as I. S. C.'s wooden cars, had become disreputable rolling wrecks. I. S. C. took over the operation of the line and virtually assumed control but not ownership.[1]

Ten new, lightweight, interurban cars were delivered in 1923 for use on these lines. Some of the replaced, older, wooden cars were brought to Fort Wayne and re-constructed as service cars and freight motors. The move to all-steel cars was started, but another serious accident involving wooden cars made an unwanted appearance.

In the evening of May 19, 1925 a westbound local car, preceeding a limited train, made an ordered meet with a pair of multiple-unit wooden cars deadheading east. Much to the surprise of the local's conductor, he noticed #306 and #307 pull out of the siding after his train had pass-ed. The two ran off to the east at a good clip - at least as far as Roanoke. There, as the duo roared in, they met car #322, a heavy steel and wood composite car, rolling out and running as the fast Wabash Valley Flyer - head on. Five people were killed in the shattering impact. The next year, in an anti-climax, car #351 provided conclusive proof as to whether steel cars were sturdier than wood. This car tangled with Union Traction's all-steel car #409. The U. T. car was so badly damaged that it had to be retired, but what could be found of the #351 was only suit-able for stove wood.

The Marion and Bluffton Traction Company had managed to keep its rail operations going and also to build up a sizable power bill with I. S. C. In need of general rehabilitation, and this power circumstance, the line was sold to I. S. C. on August 1, 1926. At the same time four more electric power companies were purchased.

This recent rail acquisition had I. S. C.'s first one-man operated interurban cars. Two light-

Top: Wooden #309, as modernized by the I. S. C. (12-24-25). Middle: The 352 remained essentially the same in exterior appearance (12-24-25). Bottom: Steel sheathed 351 was extensively rebuilt (12-24-25).

The proud display of the new steel cars for the Northern Division and the Lima line, at the Spy Run Shops, August 15, 1924.

Ex Marion & Bluffton #202 at Spy Run lettered I. S. C.

weight cars had been delivered and placed in service during 1925 on the Marion-Bluffton route. These were continued in use by I. S. C.[2]

Extensive mainline interurban rehabilitations were made in 1926. Five of the finest all-steel interurban cars ever built and two deluxe parlor-buffet cars were placed in service on such fast through runs as the "Wabash Valley Flyers". They also took over the other limited runs to leave only a few of the better wooden cars for local trips. The remaining old equipment was stored for specials and emergency use.

The Fort Wayne - Decatur Traction Company was sold to I. S. C. interests at a foreclosure sale in September 1927. The line had a dismal past and no future prospects. The total abandonment surprised no one. Killed by the then modern first class highways, the line's disappearance offered a glimpse of future happenings. Actually, I. S. C. continued to grow, while the entire industry was dying.

Indiana Service Corporation now had control of all the lines in and around Fort Wayne. They continued to purchase power companies and also to acquire a number of bus companies operating inter-city lines. In 1927, some twenty-seven intercity motor coaches were in use. Services were offered to South Bend, Warsaw, Peru, Marion, Indiana and Coldwater, Michigan. Some of these supplemented rail service but were not considered as a replacement. The phenomenal growth and expansion of I. S. C. can be attributed to the giant Insull utility interest, which gained control January 1, 1925.[3] Well over 200 miles of track were included in the system's operations.

In the downtown the interurbans shared special trackage with the city tines. This included, besides the line on Pearl Street, two large loops using Harrison, Columbia, North Clinton and Main. West of Webster Street and between Pearl and Main a three track terminal served the

The Waterloo Station and one man #326, about 1927.

Berry Street bus storage yard in October 1926. Buses are (right to left) 205, 300, 202, 112, 111, 110 and 121.

Ready for service, the new Wabash Valley Flyer sits on the ladder tracks at Spy Run Shops in 1926.

The acme of perfection in heavy, steel interurbans came with the I. S. C. 375's and 390's. The big St. Louis Car Co. built cars arrived at Spy Run in 1926 to take over all the limited and most of the local runs.

The Wabash Valley Flyer on the main line for a trial spin in the late summer of 1926.

interurban cars and intercity buses. Two converted houses served as station buildings. The passenger terminal facilities were adequate, but certainly far from impressive.

Electric freight service received better treatment. The Wabash Valley lines had recognized freight potential and participated in the Central Electric Railroads Association interchange and joint traffic arrangements. The C.E.R.A. also worked joint passenger arrangements and through fare rates.

Fort Wayne's first electric freight service was handled from the Pearl and Harrison Station. In 1906, a complete freight terminal was built west of Harrison on Pearl Street.[4] In the smaller cities freight was usually handled through the local station. The 1906 station became a very busy and crowded place as cars from many distant traction lines were always waiting loading or unloading. The business continued to grow and grow - rocketing beyond the capacity of the terminal. For years the facilities were a congested mess.

I. S. C. recognized freight as a valuable adjunct to the survival of the interurban and took steps to improve the situation. Old passenger cars were rebuilt into freight motors to speed the movement of freight cars. The old terminal was abandonded and replaced with a new terminal on the near north side. This was located on a newly built street with double tracks down its boulevard center. The Commerce Drive terminal was far superior to the old and much better than the passenger facilities. The improved handling methods, the new building and the carefully planned layout were widely hailed in the leading traction journals. Not only was service improved and speeded, through efficient handling, but additional steps were planned.[5] In 1928, tracks were built from the back of the Spy Run plant, west across North Clinton, to the interurban's Northern Division. This line had an interchange track with the New York Central and an underpass under that steam line. Other trackage was planned to reduce street running to a minimum. Special right of ways were secured, in part, around the city for these by-passes. High voltage transmission lines were also to use the land for the enlarging power business. No tracks were ever laid on this land.

The buffett section of #390 "Little Turtle" shown in a 1926 publicity photo. The service illustrated was typical.

The Fort Wayne Traction Terminal was a busy point. The special (above) was hauling a convention of men in white sheets. The view (below) about 1924, shows the rear of I. S. C. #320, ex Ohio Electric #45 (ex 87) and I. S. C. #325. Other cars are 300's and 90's. The Ohio Electric car was in I. S. C.'s Lima line service.

While the "twenties" were kind to I. S. C., the Union Traction had not been as lucky, with the real future of the interurban industry peeking through. The big U.T. fell into receivership on the last day of 1924. The company, once the epitome of good maintenance, put all its resources in passenger equipment, while the freight equipment standards fell far behind those of its economically strong northern neighbor. Consequently, I. S. C. crews soon grew to dread the thought of finding a joint operation train made up of U.T. freight equipment. This reversed an earlier picture, when everyone envied U.T.'s pioneering all-steel passenger cars and well maintained service equipment. I. S. C.'s cars seldom failed, but U.T.'s had developed habits of breakdowns, snarling traffic. Often, a freight train would arrive with only three out of four traction motors working under the big "freight motor". Control shorts produced numerous stories of freight motors wondering away from where they were parked. Other short circuits created minor fires, which threw a scare into the train crew. I. S. C. cars usually had "Golden Glow" incandescent headlights, whereas U.T. still used arc lights which were tempermental, flickering out at dark and inopportune points. An I. S. C. crew finding themselves on U.T. property at the end ot a run would go to great lengths to hide or lock up their precious headlight. These precautions saved the lamp from being "borrowed" by U.T. personnel. Arc headlights, and, on the line, plug-in telephones were considered unnecessary nuisances, which could be dispensed with. Stuck with either or both, the freight motors often made unscheduled stops on bridges so that the nuisance items could be neatly dumped in the tranquil waters below. Several old time motormen maintain that a gold mine of these items can be found deep in the waters of the rivers south of Fort Wayne. It was always easy to maintain that the light had been stolen and one less, short carbon, faltering, arc headlamp was around.

The Pearl Street freight depot during the F. W. & N. I. era. This terminal was improved but continued crowding caused it to be replaced by the new facilities.

Wabash Valley #54 on Winona R.R. trackage in Peru. In the background is an Indiana Union Traction Co. freight motor.

The new Fort Wayne freight terminal showing (above) a collection of traction freight equipment. I. S. C.'s #48 (below) leads a train on to the Commerce Drive approach tracks.

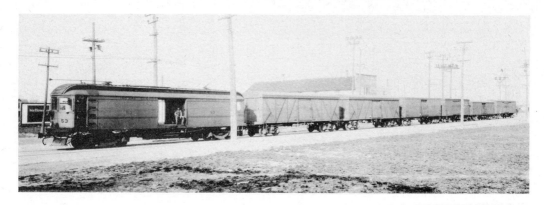

I. S. C. #53 and a six car freight train on Taylor Street in Ft. Wayne on 4-11-25. The 53 is the former 322 as first rebuilt to a freight motor.

The ever expanding Insull interests produced their biggest rail plan with the formation of the Indiana Railroad System in 1930. Interurban rail companies, unsupported by vast power holdings, had been quietly slipping into bankruptcy over the entire nation. A huge consolidation was envisioned to use the main electric lines of Indiana. Three big companies were already in the vest pocket of Midland United. These were the Northern Indiana Power Company; Public Service Company of Indiana; and, of course, the I. S. C. Missing was the Union Traction Company of Indiana, which was purchased from the receiver. The four were merged into the Indiana Railroad with the three traction-power utilities retaining individual ownership. Later, the Terre Haute, Indianapolis and Eastern Traction Company was purchased.[6] Both of the acquired properties were bought on conditions requiring the abandonment of considerable trackage prior to the sale. A unified management was expected to produce "certain economies" and generally to improve the electric railway service. New, lightweight, one-man interurban cars were put into service. Special freight delivery systems were worked out to stimulate the business that seemed threatened by highway trucks. Among the first economies of the new operators were some low rumblings about additional abandonments of more unprofitable trackage.

Power generation systems were kept by the former individual companies. Indiana Service Corporation leased to Indiana Railroad the lines of the Lafayette and Bluffton divisions, retaining control of the Northern Division and Fort Wayne City Lines. Interurban passenger and freight equipment was partly leased to the new enterprise. Indiana Railroad, also, assumed passenger service on the Northern Division with I. S. C. owned cars. All the intercity bus lines were sold or discontinued. City operations at Wabash, Peru and Logansport were retained and operated through Indiana Railroad by I. S. C., until each was abandoned.

The worn and profitless Marion-Bluffton line was torn up in August, 1931. It had been turned over to the Indiana Railroad and became one of the first links of the chain to let go. The independent Fort Wayne - Lima R.R. Co. was finally sold to the I. S. C. at foreclosure and a receiver's sale on March 16, 1933. It was abandoned and torn up immediately thus breaking the Northern, Indiana - Ohio link.

During the early 1930's more interurban companies came crashing down like thunder claps in a violent storm. Such a large number of companies fell that it became nearly impossible to record the individual abandonments. One shaky company after another became ill and died. Many large systems were also affected. Indiana Railroad was no exception, suffering heavily with the depression and the eventual collapse of Insull's Midland United holdings. Where the power division had once made up traction financial difficulties, the Indiana Railroad stood alone with no utility backing. The company failed the test of the depression. Passenger revenues nose-dived, and motor trucks gnawed steadily at the freight business. A few more years of the re-habilitation program, and the story might have been different, but . . . . ●

Two of I. S. C.'s freight motors The 859 (above) in June 1929 was at the freight terminal. The 47, later 847, at Spy Run (below) was built from an Ohio Electric passenger car.

The optimistic picture of the twenties was stripped bare with a true impression of the situation appearing. The lines were dropped in piecemeal bits as receiver Bowman Elder made retrenchments. Even before the receivership, the Lafayette Division was cut back to Peru in 1932, and some fifty-five miles of I. S. C. track work was pulled up. The remainder disappeared in September, 1938. The Bluffton Division dispatched its last car on January 19, 1941, and Indiana Railroad faded, as a traction line, with it. The era of electric interurban passenger travel to Fort Wayne was ended, not quite forty years from its inception.

The Northern Division fared somewhat better and was still partly intact. Indiana Railroad gave up passenger service on February 15, 1937, and the line was torn up back to Garrett. I. S. C. continued to operate some freight service, principally the hauling of coal to the power house, on the line until August 25, 1945. At that time the line was in such miserable condition that it was becoming very unsafe. Speed was not a consideration of this operation as the full time crew had little to do except switch a few industries.

Safety Zones appeared in Fort Wayne only on the off-center Clinton Street trackage. City car #549, heading north, was among the last group of street cars purchased.

CHAPTER 7

1920-1931

A Completely Modern Street Railway

Indiana Service Corporation had to meet the responsibility of rebuilding and re-equiping the Fort Wayne City Lines, which were always separate as an operating segment of the power company. Electric power had for some time overshadowed its early ancestry as only a part of the traction lines. Major improvements made between 1918 and 1925 included the purchase of one hundred and thirty new cars which handled all the base service. These sturdy cars were of both the single and double truck variety built to I. S. C.'s specifications and were far superior to the lightweight Birney car variations built for many medium sized city properties. No other city of comparable size could boast, in quantity, streetcars equal or superior to those in Fort Wayne. The only criticism that could be leveled at this excellent car fleet was that, in order to standardize, the same basic design was used for seven years without incorporating some of the new inovations that were developed during this period.

I. S. C. also had to rebuild and extend the city trackage. Some of the rails had been in place for over thirty years.[1] Many lines were constructed of patchwork, with rails of varying heights and weights imbedded in deteriorated paving. In carrying out this work the company promoted good public relations with informative signs and press releases. Whenever a major street rebuilding job was carried out, prominently placed signs were set up along the way explaining that I. S. C. was rebuilding a certain number of blocks at a specified cost, always followed with "just to give you better street car service." A huge electric sign downtown carried I. S. C.'s trademark, the unique script phrase "Traction-Light" which was the name used by local residents in reference to the company.

Clinton Street, between Main and Lewis, had been relaid with double track in 1910. A few years later the city widened Clinton by reducing the parkway on the east side by about ten feet. This created a serious problem for the streetcars as the tracks were well-off center. The

Double tracking of Creighton Avenue, west from Calhoun, in 1924.

Sturdy and excellent city cars were Fort Wayne's good fortune. The 536 (above) was representative of the large, new fleet of streetcars. The interior (below) view shows the neat appearance of #535.

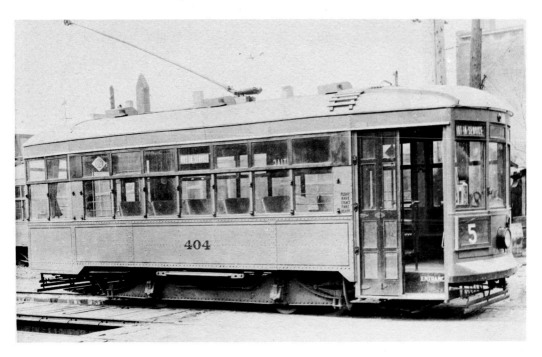

The 404, before a rear exit was added, sits on the outside pit tracks of the Baker Street yards.

Looking north on Calhoun Street toward Main Street in May, 1921. High School graduates are boarding the cars in front of the Court House.

Rebuilding the Pontiac line in August 1923. (Top) Working east from John Street, (Middle) cement mixer working at Anthony Blvd. and (Bottom) a 200 on the new track, with the temporary "shoo-fly" in the foreground, east of Weisser Park.

Southbound track was in the west side traffic lane and northbound track in the center of the street. This widening project had been undertaken to remove part of the motor vehicle traffic from the congested, parallel Calhoun Street. The move was a success from this standpoint but meant that alighting passengers, from northbound trolleys, had to be fleet of foot to reach the sidewalk in safety. To avoid serious pedestrian accidents, a series of safety islands, the only ones built in the city, were constructed for the use of the northbound cars.

The first new track work commenced in 1921 with the complete rebuilding of the tracks on Wells Street and the extension of the Huffman line south on Franklin to Third and west to Runnion. This extended line became the Third Street Line. Next, in 1922, the Lakeside line was extended east to Kensington Avenue.

Work moved forward at a quickening pace in 1923. Many of the existing lines were completely rebuilt with double-track. These included Pontiac, from Calhoun to Anthony; South Wayne, from Creighton to Kinsmoor; Calhoun from Pontiac to Rudisill; and West Creighton from Calhoun to South Wayne, which was finished in 1924. The Pontiac line was extended three times - to Plaza Drive in 1923, to Alexander in 1925, and to Queen Street in 1927.

Broadway, in 1924, was extended from Bluffton Road to Rudisill, East State was double-tracked from Spy Run to Pleasant Avenue, just west of the switch for the State School coal yard. A long freight spur was built north from the Taylor line to serve the mushrooming Dudlo Manufacturing Company. City cars also used this tackage, at shift changes, to carry the employees.

During 1924 and 1925 a long siding was built south from the Lima line, along what is now Bueter Road, to haul men and materials to the construction site of the huge International Harvester Works. In 1925 the East Lewis line was extended south on Edsall from Chestnut to Raymond by a winding route and then east to the Harvester works, where a large loop was constructed at Bueter Road. This line was planned to serve the growing new East End industrial complex and replaced the temporary siding. West Main was double-tracked and the Taylor line rebuilt in the same year.

City car 212 running around the new track work, September 25, 1923, on Pontiac Street. The track welder is being run from the overhead trolley wire.

Eastbound 202 stopping at Anthony Blvd. as workman start to rebuild the intersection.

Work motor 52 with ballast cars working on Pontiac Street west of Anthony Blvd.

New double track on South Calhoun Street in front of South Side High School. Work car #19 is just north of Oakdale Drive in 1923.

Among the many items of special equipment used was a portable saw-mill, shown here on West Creighton near Hoagland Avenue.

Two city cars with a work train, in between, during the rebuilding of the West Main Street line in 1925. Only the temporary track is in place.

West Main looking east toward Camp Allen Drive and the St. Mary's River bridge.

Single trucker 276 running around work motor 22 during the 1925 rebuilding of the West Main line.

Placing new rails in West Main Street during the rebuilding and double tracking program.

Portable cross-over on Calhoun Street, north from Douglas. Car 409 has just crossed to the east track as the 400 waits for the 510 to pass in this 1931 scene.

State Street was again extended in 1926 when it was double-tracked east of California and extended to Randalia. This was the year of least activity during the twenties.

Nineteen twenty-seven saw activity grow at a new pace as the East Washington line was completely rebuilt. The South Wayne line was extended to Maxine Avenue, where the street widened to boulevard proportions with a center parkway. Rails were laid in the street crossings as far south as Pettit in anticipation of laying tracks in the boulevard center, but the line was never extended. An isolated set of double track work was laid in the new Lafayette Street underpass, from Breckenridge to Murray, but was never connected to any line and never used.

A completely new line, Oxford, was built in 1928. The tracks were built south on Warsaw from Pontiac and then east on Oxford Street to Anthony to serve a newly developed residential area.[2]

As industries moved into the east end area the company felt the need of a second line to serve the workers. The Pontiac line, with the aid of a new underpass at Wayne Trace was extended east then north to the Lewis line at Raymond. This second line to the Harvester loop was completed in 1930.

Some of the city lines were extended at the expense of dying interurbans. The demise of the Decatur line brought an extension of service to the Calhoun line. It was extended to Cornell Circle where the interurban had branched off on to private right-of-way. A short section of the Lima line was kept for a short time to provide freight and passenger service to the Inca Manufacturing Company.

The last major trackwork was completed during 1931 and 1932. Calhoun Street was relaid with new rails from Main to Wallace. A number of unused crossovers were removed and the Baker Street turn out rebuilt. This brought most of the trackwork up to modern standards.[3]

Calhoun and Wallace where the East Creighton line turned east. This trackwork was replaced later in 1931.

Work motor 21 pushes crane car 1140 on Warsaw Street during the building of the Oxford line. The concrete poles, widely used in Fort Wayne, were made by the company.

North on Calhoun from Lewis Street. The "Traction - Light" sign can be seen on the building in the right background.

Calhoun, south from Columbia Street, in the mid thirties, with the Allen County Court House and the Lincoln Bank tower in the background.

The Spy Run yard with an assortment of car types. From left to right an 80 class trailer, a 300 series car, a 324 lightweight, city car 205, the 320, and sweeper 3. In the foreground is the ramp for unloading new cars.

The Inspection - Office building in 1929 with car 507 entering the pit area.

CHAPTER 8

The Spy Run Plant

The sale of electric power in the Wabash Valley's day had been a convenient source of extra revenue and a captive power supply for the all-important Railway Utility. To the officials of the company in those early days it was only the tail of the dog. Over the years the power business and profits consistently rose while the fortunes of the helpless interurban empire sank lower and lower. By the mid-twenties the tail was wagging the dog.

The first powerhouse in Fort Wayne had been built at Kamm Street and Spy Run Avenue. The feeder canal ran behind this property filling a large reservoir for supply to the main canal. The original plan of the Fort Wayne Water Power Company was to use this stored water and the canal to turn turbine type generators. This idea was a miserable failure and the Jenny Electric Light and Power Company installed a steam plant using this water supply and the St. Joseph River across Spy Run Avenue.

The new Spy Run powerhouse was built south of the old plant and across Kamm Street. It was opened in 1907 and subsequently enlarged in 1913, 1917 and 1925. This central station served forty-four communities, the four city lines and five interurban routes.[1] By the early 1950's it was placed on a stand-by basis and finally torn down in 1962-63.

Additional land was acquired north of the old powerhouse and this area used for material storage. The draining of the feeder canal and storage reservoir left a large low area in the rear of the property. When the city built the new Rudisill School the old building behind the powerhouse was sold to the traction company. The building was used for several purposes, including a paint shop and bus garage. The grounds were largely used for coal storage.

The former Kamm Street power building was used as a car barn until it burned September 11, 1918 with a loss of three cars. The destruction of the old building brought about a significant change. The newly created Indiana Service Corporation determined to concentrate its facilities in a complex of several buildings incorporating offices, shops and eventually replace the downtown barns. During the twenties they built a physical plant that could be rivaled by very few traction companies and certainly not surpassed by any company of equal size. The city agreed to vacate Kamm Street to the company to facilitate this.

The first new building was built in 1923 to house a paint shop, inspection pits, washing equipment and light service department on the first floor with offices on the second. Behind, to the west, the two story Engineering Building was erected. Several smaller buildings of lighter construction were put up for garaging the motor buses and service vehicles. A large car yard was constructed north of the Inspection - Office building with a long series of ladder tracks entered from Randolph Street. At the entrance a small building called the Farebox House was erected. It contained a large vault for the lockboxes brought in from arriving cars. Exit from the yard was made on Spy Run Avenue.

For some years the open cars were stored on a narrow strip of land across from the powerhouse between the street and river. They could either be run downtown or out to Robison Park as needed. This trackage was removed and a landscaped park area was created.

East elevation of the Spy Run power plant showing the 1913, 1917 and 1925 enlargements. The power house was closed in 1950's and torn down in 1963.

First power house in Fort Wayne, the Kamm Street Station was replaced by the Chestnut Street Station and the later Spy Run Station, just south of the first site. The building was used for storage of cars and materials.

Spy Run yards in 1917 showing the old power house with the new station in the rear. Work car 17 is an old city car.

The Kamm Street barn burned on September 11, 1918. The view (above) from Spy Run Ave. shows the flimsy, sheet metal construction. The Northern Division interurban car (below) was damaged in the fire.

Open cars were stored on the east side of Spy Run Ave. opposite from the power house. The Kamm Street barn stands in the background of the June, 1913 scene.

Spy Run yards and power plant, in 1925, during the expansion program.

The Inspection - Office building showing (top) the front with the ladder track exit onto Spy Run Avenue, the pit tracks (middle) and rear (bottom) view along the former Kamm Street.

The modern interurban shop building rises on the onetime reservoir site. Work car #19 pushes steam crane #1119 into position to handle heavy work.

East front of the eight track shop building, pride of the I. S. C. and envy of many other companies.

In 1925 plans were made for the dry pond section. It was filled in and the large 185' x 207' shop building constructed. This excellently equipped building became the system's main shop building and handled all repairs, rebuilding and new construction. Eight tracks entered the building which had its own yard and ladder tracks to serve it. This completed the spacious, well laid out and integrated physical plant for both power and rail facilities.

Almost coincidental with the opening of the new shops, the Huntington Shop was destroyed in a spectacular fashion. The old, main shop burned in a severe electrical storm on June 24, 1927. Lightning not only set the building on fire but also destroyed the phone lines. By the time help was summoned it was too late to save the building.

A number of substations were built to feed power to various users. At the Webster Substation current was reduced for railway, light and power. On McKinley Avenue a large substation was built to feed power to the western and southern interurbans, plus light and power in the area. Adjacent to it was the McKinley Avenue Yard with one building to house the yard office and the track and overhead departments. All ties, bricks, paving materials and poles were stored here.[2] This location was convenient to the two main lines and removed the need for hauling these materials back and forth through the city. The old wooden cars were stored in the McKinley yard and it eventually became the scrapping center of old equipment. Its usefulness dwindled with the passing years and the demise of the interurbans. It was closed and sold in the mid forties with only the substation retained.

The poorly located Glasgow Avenue barn remained on the company books for many years long after it was closed. The buildings were razed and the property sold during the twenties.[3]

As the new buildings were completed on Spy Run the facilities at Baker Street were abandoned and torn down, bit by bit. By 1930, only the one-time powerhouse remained and it was eventually sold for other uses.

Two other building assortments came to the I. S. C. with the Northern Division and the Bluffton line. The latter had a five track carbarn west of Bluffton. This had been the Marion and Bluffton's home base with complete shop facilities. The Toledo and Chicago's handsome powerhouse was closed when the line was converted to Direct Current and abandoned. A far from impressive four-track barn stood nearby. This was closed, as was the Bluffton barn, in the early thirties and torn down. The big, isolated, Boyd Park barn came to the same end. None of these buildings had much value to the system after the opening of Spy Run.

The Bluffton barn, onetime home of the Marion and Bluffton line, with freight motor 847 and a crane car with an old M. & B. passenger car behind it.

McKinley Ave. yard in the late twenties showing work equipment and surplus wooden interurban cars. Materials and supplies for the entire system were stored here.

The Kendallville barn, built as a temporary structure for the Toledo & Chicago, served as a storage barn for the I. S. C. into the mid thirties.

CHAPTER 9

1932-1962

Thirty Changing Years

Another line was planned for the developing West State Boulevard area. The first permanant city bus route was established on West State in the expectation that sufficient traffic growth would warrant a car line extension. This line was not constructed although, in anticipation of the extension, the center of the street was unpaved for years awaiting the never laid rails.[1]

No major track construction was carried on after 1931 as revenues sank. The Depression saw a rapid decrease in riding and further expansion was ended. Actual losses were incurred in only 1932, 1938 and 1940, but profits were kept at the expense of the property. Maintainance of all types was deferred and the physical appearance of the property slipped considerably. Much of the idle rolling stock deteriorated so badly that it could not be economically reclaimed. Only those cars needed in daily service were kept in good repair. In a retrenchment the lightly travelled, no. 13, Centlivre Short Line was abandoned.

In 1936, the city was finally able to complete a long awaited project for a Clinton Street underpass at the Pennsylvania - Wabash elevation. The State Highway Department participated in the work so that several Federal and State highways could be routed through the city on Clinton Street, one of the few north-south through streets. The off center car line had to go, with the Lewis Street line routed into Calhoun Street, and the Clinton tracks removed in 1937.

Probing and testing, the first street car to bus conversion occured on May 16, 1939. On that date, the single streetcar on the (#12) Jefferson "Short Line" was replaced with a motor bus. this was one of the oldest car lines, and, in the conversion, could be foreseen the end of rail operations.

By 1940, the newest streetcars were fifteen years old and no major track improvements made for nearly ten years. The company taking a good look at the trackwork, and recognizing the short comings of its aging streetcar fleet, decided to experiment in a new, but proven field - the trolley coach. Twenty-eight new trolley coaches were delivered and placed in service on July 7, 1940. Several routes were modified and changed for the new operation. Street cars were taken off the (#6) East State - Lewis, (#7) Lakeside - East Creighton and the (#9) East Washington - South Calhoun routes and the lines for the most part dismantled. The public acceptance of these new coaches was very good as the greater speed and manuevrability got the coaches through traffic quickly. The last of the four-wheeled trolleys were then removed from service.

In the changeover, most of the trolley bus lines followed the old routes. Some of the kinks and bends were straightened out by direct routing on the East Washington and the East Creighton lines. The downtown loops were equipped with double wire and continued in service. All car and coach lines were through routed, but the loops were still useful. Main and Calhoun remained the chief intersection of the city. The crossing was short one switch of being a full "Grand Union Crossing". The new trolley coach overhead was complete, allowing a coach to proceed in any direction from any approach. It was the only known installation of its kind.

Rails were left in place to reach the three High Schools. This included about ten blocks on Calhoun south of Pontiac, to reach South Side High School, and one block on Lewis to reach

Three brand new Yellow Coach buses, 600 - 602, in front of the State School on East State Blvd. in 1929.

A 1936 view (above) of 504 in need of paint. The new paint scheme of maroon and cream is shown (below) on 534, in front of the Allen County Court House in November 1937.

Night scene on Calhoun Street with single truck car 441 going north on the Lakeside run, about 1938.

The 551 at the end of the Broadway line. Foster Park and the St. Mary's River are in the background. The color scheme and design were modified in 1940 and the company name again appeared.

Private right-of-way under the Wabash R. R. built for the Lima line was also used by the Lewis-Harvester line until 1940.

Car 545 turning into the Harvester Loop. Pontiac - Harvester #5 Line cars were run as trippers only, after the Third Street end of the route was dropped.

Newest single trucker, #449, in the snow on the Jefferson line. Only one car was used to operate the line.

North from the Transfer Corner, Main and Calhoun, in 1943 showing the trackwork and trolley coach overhead in place.

Central High School. North Side High School could still be reached by the remaining East State Blvd. trackage retained for freight. Student passenger volume was too large for the number of available buses. Consequently school trippers and sports events required the streetcars.

Following the initial success of the new vehicles, forty more trolley coaches were ordered and delivered in 1942. Plans were made for the immediate conversion of all remaining street car lines to trolley coaches. Wires for the new vehicles were placed on all routes when an unexpected wartime development appeared. The Office of Defense Transportation sent orders to all transit companies with servicable rail vehicles to make all possible use of them and conserve rubbertired vehicles. This order applied directly to Fort Wayne, where, although all the new wire was strung, the remaining rail lines were in servicable condition. Trolley cars were to continue for at least the duration on these lines, except (#5) Third Street, which was converted in 1943, when the elderly Wells Street bridge was condemned for heavy vehicles. Pontiac, the other end, was also switched to trolley coach with street cars operating as trippers.

This latter route had a long stretch of private right-of-way in a thinly-populated area, with right angle turns at either end. For years, motormen on the late evening runs, anticipating no fares, would put the controller in a low position and catch a short nap. The car would lazily swing along and drift into the curve with enough roll to wake the sleeper. At least once the car leaned a little too far dumping the whole thing on its side. No doubt an interesting alibi was produced by the rudely awakened motorman.

During the war years a unique combination service appeared with some lines using both vehicle types. Under normal circumstances, rails and rubber are not compatible. For the passengers, this service was a blessing in disguise as Fort Wayne did not experience the equipment

Streetcars and trolley coaches used the same overhead. Car 538 is turning south from Main to Calhoun on the Broadway - South Wayne line.

A busy fall day on Calhoun Street at Washington in 1941. Car 536 is heading south to the Oxford line.

shortage which was keenly felt in many cities. The wartime demands created a motorman, or driver, shortage and some woman were hired to close this gap in personnel. The (#8) West Main - Oxford, (#4) South Wayne - Broadway lines remained as street car lines with occasional trolley coach service. The (#11) Belt Line, which was used for special service, was also equipped for both vehicles. The rider could not be certain which vehicle type might convey him to his destination. Fortunately, the later conversion plans had called for almost identical routes following the old street car lines. The (#10) Taylor line had been changed to motor buses in 1940 and was in part dismantled from the end, at Ardmore Avenue back to McKinley Ave. The remainder had been left in place to move cars to McKinley yard for scrapping. When the O. D. T. order arrived, the car line received a new lease on life as streetcar service was restored as far as McKinley Avenue with a motor bus operating the outer end.

The suspension of hostilities brought an early end to restrictions and the delayed modernization program was pushed ahead with an early end to street cars anticipated. Equipment deliveries, however, were on a long-term basis which created a delay. Another factor was the population increase which meant that additional equipment was needed to close the remaining gap for complete conversion from rails to rubber.

Sunday, September 9, 1945, was a quiet day on all street car routes when, for the first time in seventy-three years, except for two service stopping strikes and the Great Epizootic, not a street car operated. Full schedules were operated that Sunday, and every Sunday, with buses. Fewer and fewer cars were seen on week days, unless one passed the Spy Run yards where over forty tired street cars rested quietly. Over ninety per cent of the vehicles miles were operated by trolley coaches and motor buses. Some street cars still clanged forth to fill the rush hour gap.

Rattling over the St. Mary's River, 532 holds down the rescued Taylor Street line in 1942. Both bridges have since been replaced.

Car 543 rumbles off the Wells Street bridge shortly before the line was changed to trolley coaches. A single, off center, track was used to cross the old bridge.

Tripper car 504, on Clinton Street turning on the Main, Clinton, Columbia and Calhoun loop to return to the South Wayne route.

Special cars on East State Blvd. with cars 541 and 531 waiting a load near North Side High School. This was the remaining East State trackage to the State School after the line was changed to Trolley coaches.

The 539, on the Third Street run and a trolley coach crossing the Nickle Plate R.R. tracks on Calhoun Street in 1942.

End of the line. The Taylor line (#10) wyed at the entrance of the old McKinley yards. Many cars that entered here never returned as this was the principal scrapping point.

All the remaining streetcars and their replacements, the trolley coaches, stand together in the Spy Run yards. This was June 1947 and the end was close at hand.

The inevitable deliveries of new equipment were completed in the late spring of 1947 and spelled the finale for the remaining street car lines. On the evening of June 27, 1947, I. S. C. Transportation Vice President Donald H. Walker shook hands with honorary conductor Frank Carbaugh and sent the last car on it way. Mr. Carbaugh had been a conductor on the first day of electric cars in Fort Wayne and requested permission to ride the last. It seemed fitting that he ride the first and last time and he was fitted out in a uniform and made a conductor again. This was the first conductor on a city car in twenty-five years. The ceremonies were very brief with few realizing that an era had closed. Later that night, with little fanfare, car #543 rumbled back to Spy Run Shops for the last time as seventy-five years of rail passenger service came to a close.

Passenger transportation continued rolling on rubber tires although the final chapter of the rail service was yet to come. Indiana Service Corporation in this change carried out it's requirement to get its transit facilities in order and now proceeded to dispose of them to comply with the Securities and Exchange Commission orders.

American Gas and Electric (now American Electric Power) disolved I. S. C. by merging the power facilities into it's subsidiary, the Indiana & Michigan Electric Company and offering the city transit lines for sale. These were sold to a local group of business men in May 1948, headed by Donald H. Walker. They formed a new corporation, Fort Wayne Transit, Inc., with Walker as President and local ownership returned after a half century abscence. The well known phrase of "Traction - Light" disappeared as one became two.

Nominal title to the rails, still in place, on Spy Run and East State Blve., remained with Fort Wayne Transit. This trackage was the last vestige of the once far flung traction freight service and was used for hauling freight and coal cars from the New York Central to the City Filtration Plant, State School and Centlivre Brewery. Two of the old freight motors had been retained in servicable condition by Indiana-Michigan Electric Company, but one, the #848, was soon retired. Actual trackage amounted to about sixteen blocks of street operation or 1.4 miles. Fort Wayne Transit, by contract agreement, maintained the track and overhead and did the repair work on #817, the aging switch motor. Finally, on March 30, 1952, other arrangements were made, and this last fragment of rail operation was ended.

June 27, 1947 saw #543 make the last streetcar run. The patronizing sign was typical of the era when many transit companies switched from streetcar to buses.

Switching motor #817 at the Centlivre Brewery. This is the trackage that originally led to the Robison Park line and was later the Centlivre Short line.

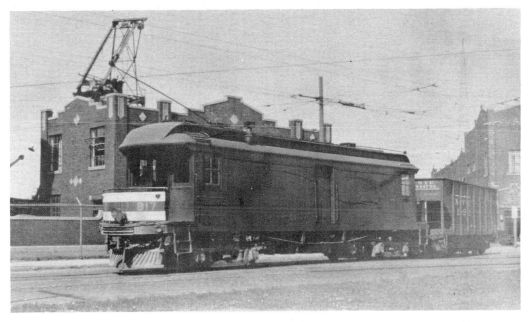

Switching on Spy Run Avenue with 817 at the power plant in Indiana & Michigan days during May 1950.

Following the war, and in keeping with the modernization program, ten trolley coaches and thirty motor buses were added to the fleet. In 1951, the company purchased more motor buses which were to use propane gas instead of gasoline. Their successful operation caused the entire fleet to be converted to propane and this fuel was used on subsequent motor bus purchases. Propane gas had several definite advantages over gasoline including reduced maintenance and a lower price.

The conversion of the East Washington line to motor buses posed a problem as the company now had a surplus of trolley buses and a shortage of motor buses. The company acquired a number of recent model motor buses and sold its newest trolley buses.

Construction was started late in 1953 to build new offices and garage facilities on Leesburg Road in western Fort Wayne. This new plant was completed in 1954 and consolidated all the company's operations. The modern and complete garage replaced the Spy Run operations where servicing had been carried out in the old interurban shop building.

Early in 1959, with no fanfare, wires were removed from the South Calhoun line. Shortly afterward Fort Wayne Transit began to receive a number of used motor buses from Detroit. Later that same year wires were removed from the Lakeside, East Creighton, State and Lewis lines and the public became aware that some changes were being made by the transit company. In March of 1960 the Third Street and Pontiac lines were also changed to motor buses leaving four trolley bus lines. During this period about thirty-five of the older trolley buses were scrapped. In June 1960 the remaining lines were changed to motor bus and electric power ceased to be the prime mover in Fort Wayne.

Several factors brought on this conversion but the principal one was the necessity to extend the lines. The needed wire extensions would have been very expensive and would have committed the company to the purchase of newer trolley buses, a luxury few privately owned transit companies can afford. The explosion of the city's boundaries would have made route selection very difficult with fixed facilities. Another problem was the 600 volt D.C. power which the power company preferred to stop. The transit company was the last customer for this voltage and the antique coverting equipment was most uneconomical.

Main and Calhoun looking east, in 1956, showing Fort Wayne Transit Company's trolley coach operation. The overhead wires here allowed a trolley to turn in any direction which was an extremely rare installation.

November 1960 and the last Fort Wayne trolley coach is handed over by Mr. D. H. Walker (left) to Dick Haupt (center) of the Allen County - Fort Wayne Historical Society. Others include Harley Graham and George Bradley for the Jaycees.

Without wires, the 157 was towed by a truck tractor to storage awaiting future exhibit.

Fort Wayne Transit's Leesburg Road office and garage building were completed in 1954 consolidating the city transportation operations.

Finding no customers for the used trolley buses Fort Wayne Transit decided to scrap them. Unfortunately no one had had the foresight to preserve one of the street cars for historical purposes which was much regreted by the Allen County - Fort Wayne Historical Society. Mr. Walker offered one of the trolley buses to the Historical Society and the Fort Wayne Junior Chamber of Commerce offered to prepare it for display purposes in the park next to the museum. The Park Board politely declined this offer as they felt it had no immediate appeal and and that it would be a distinct liability. Consequently, the forward thinking Historical Society and Jaycees stored this remaining vehicle, the last in Indiana, until such time as it may be placed on display.

Fort Wayne Transit is continuing its agressive program to best serve the riding public. Service extensions are made wherever any potential appears. Such progressive operations are not often found in the city transportation industry today. The company remains with the same problem facing all transit firms as the continued growth of auto ownership casts its cloud on the future prospects, but the increase in traffic congestion makes mass transportation still more necessary for any large city. Fort Wayne Transit has been able, so far, to operate with fares under those of all other major Indiana cities. If the continued efforts of the transit company, city administrators, traffic engineers and merchants can find a way to speed transit operations, there may well be a return to public transit usage by enough people tired of fighting traffic so that the downward trand of riding in evidence since World War II may yet be reversed.

CHAPTER 10

The Small City Lines

City street cars were operated in five of the cities served by the interurban. These were Huntington, Peru, Wabash, Logansport and Lafayette. The Lafayette lines continued to use street cars until 1940, although it became an independent company in 1920.

All of these systems were in operation at the time of the 1904 consolidation with some extensions made shortly afterwards. For a brief period a city car ran in Huntington, but it used only the interurban trackage, which was not suited for a city line and by 1910 it had been suspended.

Wabash was fortunate because the Wabash River Traction Co. had laid out a small city system as part of their lines. It was in full operation by 1901 with the 3.1 miles of track continued by the successor company. The trackage was reduced to 2.4 miles when a short section paralleling the interurban, on the south side of the river, was torn up. The trackage might be best described as being in the form of a cross with lines roughly reaching the four points of the compass. The east-west rails were used by the interurban and the north-south by the city line. The city line was single track with a passing siding located, in the most unlikely place, in the center of the Wabash River bridge. With only two cars in use passing was not a serious problem! Operations were continued until August 31, 1931. Revenues were down and the trackage in disrepair. Indiana Railroad substituted motor buses as an experiment but these were withdrawn on April 1, 1933. Indiana Railroad had operated the line for I. S. C. after 1930, but it still belonged to I. S. C.

Last day of operation, August 31, 1931, in Wabash, Indiana with #214 going down the hill on Wabash Street.

One man car #180, in Wabash, on Wabash Street at Market Street during the mid twenties. Newer cars of the 200 class soon replaced these old deck roof types.

Wabash River Traction's #13 near the city limits of Peru. The location is East Main Street shortly after the line opened.

Fort Wayne & Wabash Valley's #133 at the Chesapeake and Ohio Ry. crossing on West Main Street in Peru, about 1910.

PERU CITY LINES

The Peru City Lines were the smallest, but they lasted longer than the other small town properties. The eastern portion of the line was opened in 1901 and the western section in 1904. The cars ran entirely on interurban trackage which entered the city on East Main Street and ran out on West Main. This provided a 1.8 mile stretch that was ideal for a small operation with cars running from the heart of the town in two directions.[2] Connections were made in the downtown with the Union Traction, Co., from the south, and the Winona line, from the north. The Winona ran a city car on its trackage for a short period starting in 1909.

When the interurban was cut back in 1932 the West Main line was kept for the exclusive use of the city cars, although Indiana Railroad's interurbans continued to roll on East Main. The small cars continued to ply the east-west route until December 8, 1934 when all city service was suspended. Again Indiana Railroad ran the city line for I. S. C. after 1930.

LOGANSPORT CITY LINES

Logansport, as a county seat and an area center, had grown to a size big enough to support a street railway by 1880. The Logansport Street Railway Co. was chartered in 1882 to build two routes. The cars were pulled by horses and might have continued as such for a number of years except for a disaster in the summer of 1891.

Plans for electrification were being considered when the car barn burned with all the rolling stock. It is not clear whether service was completely suspended or not, but from all indications horse cars were borrowed until October 1, 1891 when electrification was completed. The company was recapitalized as the Logansport Railway Company.

Downtown Peru, Indiana with I. S. C. #206 heading west on Main Street. With only one line, destination signs were not needed.

Broadway, in Logansport, Indiana about 1910. An interurban passenger car, with a trailer, a freight motor and four city cars are in a traffic tie-up.

Double truck open car #370 and four open trailers at Spencer Park in Logansport.

The line was rebuilt and extended when the Wabash Valley system took over. They included the city trackage built by the proposed Logansport, Rochester and Northern Traction Company. This brought the city operated mileage to 12.5 miles.[3]

Financially, the line's revenues started a severe drop in 1913 with increasing losses. An attempt was made at one-man cars as an economy and wartime measure in 1916 but it started an unpleasant chain of events.

Local employees struck the company and their sympathizers got out of hand with serious consequences. Afraid that the situation might be too much for the local law enforcement officers the company put the cars away and stopped operating. The power was cut off and the interurbans stopped for fear of damage. Striking linemen diverted power from the Union Traction interurban power lines and ran out a couple of cars. These cars were badly damaged as they were run up and down the streets. Some of the overhead wire was also pulled down. Three days later organized authority seemed to regain control and services were restored under police protection.

A boycott remained in effect for some time but a peaceful settlement was finally worked out. One of the agreements required the company to put the trackage back in good condition and furnish new cars. Logansport city officals were very touchy about being part of the tail on the Fort Wayne kite with nothing but cast-off equipment. Ten new one-man cars identical to the new Fort Wayne single truckers were placed in service. This seemed to sooth everyone and revenues took a significant upswing.

Revenues began to decline in the late twenties with small losses being recorded. Indiana Railroad was nominally in charge after 1930, although the lines and cars belonged to I. S. C. When Indiana Railroad proposed the abandonment of the Peru - Lafayette interurban the fate of the city line was sealed. Neither firm was interested in an isolated street car system which again needed extensive track reconstruction. The city service was completely suspended, without bus substitution, on April 29, 1932, and the interurban removed on June 22, 1932.

The Lafayette lines were controlled by the Fort Wayne systems from 1903 until 1920. This company's history is a story in itself and well recorded in Mr. Dave Chambers, "LAFAYETTE STREET RAILWAYS".

All the city lines were kept as separate entities by the central accounting department. As separate accounts all fixed charges, revenues, equipment, depreciation, etc. could be charged to the several lines and a profit or loss record maintained. In all the cities except Peru the interurban was treated as a foreign company and rentals paid to the city accounts. In Peru, where the city cars used the interurban trackage exclusively, the Peru City Lines were classed as the foreign company and the interurban, oddly enough, considered the home company.[4]

The Logansport car barn was the best small city facility on the system.

One of the ten new cars purchased in 1918 to revitalize the city lines, #298 runs through downtown Logansport about 1925.

CHAPTER 11

Rolling Stock

Unfortunately no accurate or detailed records of the rolling stock exist prior to the 1920 Inventory. Many of the old records were disposed of as the company changed hands. However, several general accounts from the earlier periods are available, allowing a reasonably complete picture. Unfortunately, all but two of the opens were scrapped before 1920. About 1900, Fort Wayne Traction established a fairly uniform numbering system which continued through the successor companies.

Two horsecars arrived in Fort Wayne on January 5, 1872 and were immediately followed by two more. These may have been built by the J. M. Jones or John Stephenson Companies. Four more were added soon after and included at least one open car. Eight cars were in use in 1876 and the company is presumed to have had ten, numbered 10-19. Photographs of #14 and #16 show them to have been sturdy, six-window, cars. They were double end and usually pulled by one horse. They were prominently numbered and carried the name "Citizens' Street R.R. Co." Two more cars were acquired in November 1884, although the numbers are unknown. A snow plow arrived in 1886.

Fort Wayne Street Railroad purchased nineteen cars in 1888. Route names now replaced the the company name on the car sides. These cars were twelve feet long and had four large windows. They appeared smaller and lighter than the earlier cars. Numbers become confused at this point as a different number #16 appears in a photo. It is a sister to a known car numbered thirty-one. It is quite probable that some of the old cars were repainted and renumbered.

These first cars were seventeen years old and some may have been scrapped or destroyed. Evidence of some cars disappearing appeared in December 1888, when the company reported twenty-eight cars in use for base service. A minimum of twenty-nine are known to have existed by this date. As the city was experiencing considerable growth, new horse cars were added. The only record shows new cars which were purchased in March 1891. These may have been the six window cars numbered in the thirties. By July 1892 the total number was about fifty, a small drop, indicating the probable end of the remaining 1871 cars.

In June 1892 three new electric cars arrived on the Nickel Plate and were unloaded at the Glasgow Avenue barns. These included seventeen open and sixteen closed cars built by J. M. Jones Co. of Troy, New York. Each was equipped with a Dorner truck. The closed cars had open platforms. Known numbers of these sixteen foot cars are #24, 26, 28, 30, 34, 36 and 38. The total number delivered seems to have been forty closed, 2 through 80 (even numbers only), and twenty open. A sprinkler was added in 1893. The horse cars were sold, although one seven-bench open may have been electrified and used for about three years.

The 1894 purchase of the Centlivre line brought some more horsecars into Fort Wayne Electric Railway's ownership. The bill of sale included twenty horses, three summer cars, five closed cars, thirty sets of harness, three extra car trucks and an assortment of horse collars, picks, bars and brooms. The closed cars were numbered 1 through 5. The horsecars were used for less than two months by the new owners. These cars, from an unknown builder, were only

Fort Wayne Traction's #14 was probably one of the first sixteen cars purchased for the initial electricication in 1892. These cars were all retired before 1914.

Eight bencher, open car #35, somewhere on the Main Street line, advertises a City Band concert at Centlivre's Park about 1895.

J. M. Jones built #117, and its business appearing Peckham truck, in Fort Wayne Traction Company livery.

Nine bencher #95 pausing for a moment on the return from Robison Park, around the turn of the century.

seven years old and were undoubtedly sold. Some of these, and other retired Fort Wayne horsecars, are believed to have been sold to smaller midwestern cities.

The perplexing number system is confused at this point as all the eight-bench open cars carried odd numbers. A new state law in 1895, ordered enclosed vestibules on all closed cars. Some of the cars were single end operation at first with only one end closed. All except the summer cars, were later closed and made double end. Many of the very popular open cars were added to the fleet bringing the total of open motors and trailers to about fifty. Jones continued as the builder for these electric cars, numbered 1 through 85 (odd numbers only). Fort Wayne Consolidated bought twenty-five nine-bench cars, #87 - 135 (odd numbers only).[1]

Cincinnati built 148 at Emrick's switch in West Lafayette near the site of the present Purdue Field House.

One of the home built cars #130, at the Glasgow Avenue barns, about 1904.

With the exception of the latter group, all were numbered together whether motorized or not. Two and even three car trains of opens ran on the Robison Park line. The open cars carried their numbers in the clerestory windows. Few companies bothered with replacing such numbers when mass renumberings took place. The opens carried their original numbers to the end although newer closed cars also had the same numbers. Such a system, no doubt, posed many problems.

Fort Wayne Traction's expansion of the city system required additional closed cars. They acquired several groups of large single truck, deck roof, closed cars. The first came from J. M. Jones, in 1902, and although the total built is unknown at least ten, possibly twenty, were ordered with numbers ranging from #109 to #119. One definite stray was numbered 133 and it is possible that a second group was delivered following the intervening home built cars.

The company's Baker Street Shops produced the #121-131 class. They were sturdy and bulky appearing straight-sided cars. These cars and the Jones cars were mounted on Peckham trucks which were popular at the time.

Cincinnati Car Company and the Barney and Smith Company built the #140-156 series for the Fort Wayne and Wabash Valley lines. They were numbered together in one group and the exact builder of each one is unknown. Most of them were later switched to a Curtis truck. The Cincinnati built cars had five large windows whereas the Barney and Smith group had eight smaller windows. The B. & S. cars definitely known were #140, 141 and 145. Known Cincinnati cars were #144, 146, 147, 148, 149, 150, 154, 155, 156. There is no explanation for the odd and confusing numerical system applied to these early car groups.

The #169 was a stray built by the St. Louis Car Company as the pilot model of a proposed order. Little is known about the car although it was in service for about seventeen years.

Between 1907 and 1909 Cincinnati Car built two more groups of single truck closed cars, which may be considered the second generation as they replaced the original closed cars. These were deck roofed semi-convertible cars. The first, #170-175, had a Peckham truck while #176-201 had a Curtis truck, next to achieve popularity on the system.

The creation of the Wabash Valley system produced a varied collection of city cars from the several underlying properties. The small, older cars of these companies were done away with and probably sold, as they had useful life left in them. Most of Lafayette Street Railway's and Wabash River Traction's single truck opens were numbered into the existing Fort Wayne open group. Lafayette had seventeen Brill built eight-bench cars very similar to those already owned. These, however, may have been sold. Wabash River Traction had five ten-bench opens with partitions separating the platforms from the rest of the car. These, it is believed, became #64-68. They were not used in Fort Wayne being most generally used in the original locations. Some of these were wrecked in the collapse of the Boyd Park Barn. The total of opens soared to over seventy.

The other strays included two, double truck, fifteen-bench opens which were built as number 12 and 13 for Wabash River Traction. The two were re-numbered 370-371 and used principally on the four small properties. Their large capacity made them profitable for special movements although they required a conductor after one-man operation was established.

The 250's were six, double truck, closed cars built by American Car Company and two groups existed. The #250-251, believed 10-11 on Wabash River Traction were used on the Battleground line. This pair was mounted on Peckham trucks. The other four were Wabash River Traction's cars and had probably been numbered 14-17 riding on McGuire trucks. Double truck city cars were not popular in Fort Wayne and these were infrequent visitors to the Summit City. One car, usually #254 or #255, held a run on the Robison Park line. During the winter months three round trips were made each day and a heavy, double truck car was needed to break through the snow on the long suburban line. Two were kept for similar reasons in Lafayette. Two of the group found their way into work service in 1910 as line cars #40 and #41. The other one pro-

Winding up her years #191, an old Cincinnati built two-man car, poses for a record shot prior to scrapping.

bably ended as a work car also.

The "nearside" and "P. A. Y. E." (Pay as you enter) systems hit Fort Wayne simultaneously with a single truck variety produced for the system. Twenty-six of these were built by Cincinnati Car Co. and J. G. Brill Co. The #202-220 were true nearsides and single end operated. As such, they were limited in Fort Wayne to those lines which had turn around facilities. During the late teens the city lines were extended and most of the numerous "Wyes" were removed making double-end cars a necessity. After only a few years service these cars had the stubby rear end rebuilt to full platform size, doors added and converted to double-end operation. Thus rebuilt the cars gave many years of service.

The #221-227 were typical, single truck, Brill, standard nearsides. These "muzzle-loaders" were built specifically for use in Lafayette. They were well suited for the long line linking the city to Purdue University and West Lafayette across the Wabash River. This line had two large loops at either end, ideal for these cars. When the Lafayette system was separated the cars came back to Fort Wayne. One of these was treated the same as the low 200's, made double-end and considerably rebuilt. It is doubtful that the others were rebuilt as I. S. C. listed all but #225 scrapped by 1922. Double-end #225 was in service at Spy Run in 1926 and, in 1928 it was run to Garrett where it ended its years at the Vandalia interlocking plant. Still mounted on its truck it sat on a couple of rails by the interurban tracks.

The official inventory, which did not give car numbers, of Fort Wayne and Northern Indiana Traction rolling stock as of December 31, 1918 indicates poor records, poor memory, or intentional ommission of several cars. This report was prepared primarily for fare increase requests and impending receivership.[2] I. S. C's 1920 Appraisal and Inventory was for an entirely different purpose, primarily to raise the book value of assets to the highest possible valuation. The overlooked equipment, servicable or not, re-appeared on the lists. If the useless and now scrapped opens had still been on the property they would have been listed.[3]

The 1920 inventory showed the past twenty years as quite hard on the company's cars. Many cars were missing. The #142, 143, 151,152 and 153 were missing from the 1904 group. The #183, 189 and 195 had disappeared from the 1909 purchases and #203 was gone from the 1913 near-sides. Most of the older groups were nearly gone with only a few remaining while

The Taylor Street line shortly after the Wabash Valley Company started using it for a city route, with #172 in front of the American Steel Dredge Co. office.

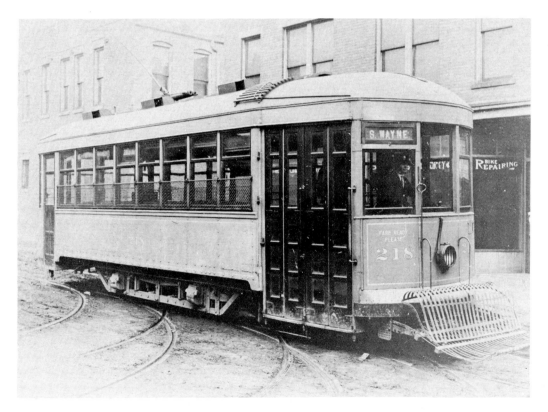

One of the first group of "nearsides", #218 was placed in service in 1913 and is shown on the lead tracks to the Chestnut Street barns. These cars were later rebuilt for double end operation and the rear door was removed.

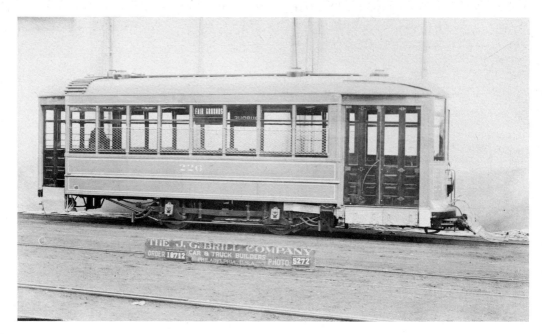

Nearside car #226 was built for use in Lafayette, Indiana; one of the small companies owned by the Fort Wayne company. It later saw some service in Fort Wayne.

The Vandalia interlocking plant on the Northern Division, south of Garrett. Car 225 was taken out of service in 1928 and used to replace an earlier wooden tower.

Nearside #216 and work car #13 on the outside pit tracks on the south side of Chestnut Street in 1920.

some classes were completely intact. Some of these were victims of the fires in the Kossuth Street barn at Lafayette, Kamm Street barn in Fort Wayne and the Boyd Park tornado.

Fort Wayne and Northern Indiana purchased ten large double truck cars in 1917. Numbers 240-249 were two-man, rear entrance cars and the typical, arch roof, steel design of the period was adhered to in this group. The need for a large capacity car on certain lines and the economy that might be achieved was being noticed.

With the proposal to change to one-man operation the company felt it would be cheaper to buy new equipment than to invest large sums in rebuilding the antiquated cars. Twenty-five single truck, one-man cars were delivered in 1918 receiving numbers 275-299. Cars #291-299 were the first to arrive and are believed to be the only ones, of this group, mounted on Curtis trucks with the rest on St. Louis #113 trucks. This same group of nine was sent to Logansport to upgrade the car lines. The following year thirty-five more similar cars were delivered and numbered #400-434.

I. S. C. had a large number of cars on its hands when it assumed control. Standarization did not exist and several operational types were on the property. The simplest solution was to purchase more new cars, recondition the newer ones and dispose of the balance. Sixty, improved, double and single truck cars, following the basic design of the recent purchases were added in the next three years (#510-554 and #435-449). This move created Fort Wayne's third and last generation of street cars. The 240's were rebuilt to #500-509 and the #275-289 #400-435 had rear exits added. All the single truck cars in these groups were placed on the St. Louis 113 truck. One hundred and thirty modern city cars now served the system.

By 1926 over ninety, old, cars were retired from service. These were all closed cars with the exception of the last two opens #370-371.[4]

Although a specific truck type is given for each car class some variations appear with certain fairly standard types adopted during different periods. Trucks were freely switched from one car to another so that an occasional photo will show a car with what appears to be the wrong truck. Some experimental trucks were also used. These included a set of Timken-Detroit "automotive drive" trucks used under car #523 in 1930 and a set of Standard, interurban light-weight trucks used on #325 for a short while.

The 504, as rebuilt to a one man car, in October 1923, on East State Blvd. This shows the sand and maroon color scheme.

The first group of new single truck cars appeared in 1918. These were built by St. Louis Car Co. and were far superior to the Birney cars used in many cities.

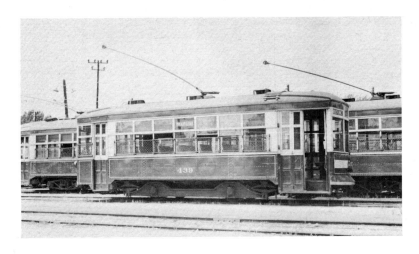

Top: The last group of single truck cars came in 1922. The 439 in new paint in 1936. Middle: The 290's, from Logansport, did not have rear exits added and were stored after Peru service ended. A number of cars stored cars fell in great disrepair and were scrapped. Bottom: I. S. C. experimented with #508, by blocking off the upper window sash. The operation was not repeated and this car went to Cornwall, Ontario in 1945.

Timken light weight "automotive drive" trucks were tried under #523. The experiment was not repeated after the brakes set the car on fire.

Steam powered, boom derrick, #1119 and a freight motor on the south side of the Inspection - Office building at the Spy Run shops in 1924. This was formerly Kamm Street, vacated by the city to I. S. C.

The last color scheme and stripping was adopted in 1940, as applied to #542. This basic pattern was used on the trolley buses and motor buses until pastel green invaded the scene in 1962.

Maintenance and service equipment included a wide variety of types. Several sweepers and snow plows were on the lists as well as a sprinkler. A number of old city cars were rebuilt for various uses by the track and line departments. These included, among others, a cement mixer on an old Peckham truck and the rather unlikely, electric powered, portable, circular saw. A fair size, rail bound, steam shovel, was used for street construction. In 1926, the company purchased a new, electric derrick car to replace its old, steam-powered, boom crane.

Little change took place in the city car equipment after the mid-twenties except the continuous reduction of numbers as the single truck cars were scrapped. A number of the 500 series cars were sold to other companies to meet wartime equipment shortages.

Cornwall Street Railway, of Cornwall, Ontario purchased two in 1945. For some reason they bought two cars of a different type. The #508, which was the only car with the upper windows plated over was one of the oldest, double truck cars. They also bought #516 which was from the second group and although these cars basically looked the same they had many differences. The cars were renumbered #33 and #37 respectfully and retained the same paint scheme in Cornwall. Both were scrapped when Cornwall abandoned their trolleys.

Two cars were sold to St. Petersburg, Florida in 1942 to ease a car shortage. These were the #506 and #507 which became #118 and #119 at their new home. They presented a pleasing contrast to the wooden seat, double truck birneys used in St. Petersburg. Buses were substituted as soon after the war as possible and these cars were junked.

Atlantic City Transportation Company had modernized their fleet with single end Brilliners before the war and disposed of most of their double end cars. This company was unique in having only one, but extremely long, car line serving several adjoining shore communities. During the frequent conventions, schedules were totally disrupted as very few looping facilities were available for the Brilliners. Medium size, double-end cars were needed to maintain traffic whenever a parade broke the line in two. For some reason they decided to buy six war weary

Interior of a 510 class car taken at the Harvester Loop. The sign board is letter "Harvester" on one side and the other side lettered "Alexander St. Only", a turn back crossover.

Ready to return to the South Wayne half of the #4 line, #544 sits at the end of the Broadway line. This 1945 picture shows the high standard of maintainance on the I. S. C.

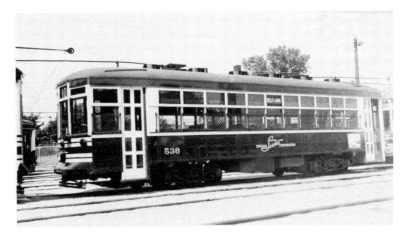

Three variations of the 500 series double truck cars. The 501 (top) was rebuilt from the 1917 cars, the 518 (middle) is from the 510-524 series and the 538 (bottom) is from the 525-539 series.

Top: Cornwall St. Ry. #37, ex Fort Wayne 516 at the Cornwall Ontario barn. Middle: St. Petersburg, Florida #119 was Fort Wayne #507. Bottom: Atlantic City Transportation Company's #298 was Fort Wayne's #550.

cars in 1945 from Fort Wayne. These were #527, 537, 540, 546, 550 and 552 which became #294-299 at Atlantic City. They were not heavily used and with one exception scrapped by the mid 1950's outliving their sisters by a number of years. One car outlasted all the Atlantic City cars and was not junked until 1958, although it had been out of service for some time.

Fort Wayne Transit's present operating fleet is comprised of post war motor buses, of varying ages, built by the Twin Coach Company. The body styles and seating capacity varies slightly but essentially all are the same. All those purchased new or used before 1957 are propane gas powered. The later acquisitions, from Detroit, Michigan and Buffalo, N. Y., are nearly identical but use gasoline for fuel. These were augmented by a group of G. M. C. diesel buses acquired in 1962.

The trolley buses were built by the J. G. Brill Company. Sixty-eight of these vehicles were delivered to I. S. C. in 1940 and 1942. Those purchased in 1940 seated 40 passengers and were numbered 100-127 while the larger 1942 group, 128-167 seated forty-four. Ten more were purchased in 1946, 168-177, from ACF-Brill Co. This group was sold to Indianapolis Railways Co. in 1953. The last trolley buses were removed from service June 10, 1960 and with one exception, were all scrapped by December 1960. The remaining coach, #157, has been stored for a future permanant historical exhibit.

During the twenties an assorted collection of bus types was gathered together as I. S. C. bought up small bus lines. These ranged from fancy Fageol parlor coaches to workhorse Internationals, Whites and Reos. Some of these were eventually worked into temporary city service, with the Whites giving some service in Logansport. City buses, of the so-called conventional type, were purchased from Fargo, Studebaker and Yellow Coach.

The oldest, and oddest buses were numbered in the thirties. The body amounted to a windowed box mounted on a small truck chassis. These had longitudinal seats as in early street cars and large, hard-rubber tires.

Standardization, for years unheard of, and later attemped in the twenties on the newer street cars has been successfully achieved by Fort Wayne Transit with one basic bus type.[5]

City bus #33, placed in service by F. W. & N. I. Tr. Co., on West Main Street in 1916.

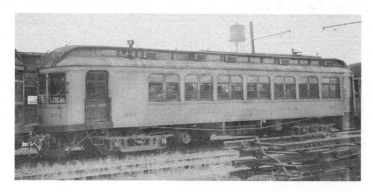

Wooden cars in storage at the McKinley Yards. (1) 301 as repainted by I. S. C. (2) 309, a second series car, on Curtis trucks. (3) 352, one of the original limited cars. (4) 302 and 303 in the scrap line.

The oldest interurban cars were built for the Fort Wayne and Southwestern as #301-305 by John Stephenson Car Company in 1901. These 43 ft. cars were combines with an express-baggage section forward. At least three more short double end passenger cars were added soon afterwards to handle the traffic on the Wabash extension. These were apparently Jackson and Sharp products and numbered from #205, although the exact numbers are unknown. Car #205 is the only known car relettered "Fort Wayne, Logansport, Lafayette and Lima Traction Co." It was barely long enough for its lengthy title.

As the Wabash Valley system was molded it was obvious that the small interurban and suburban cars used on the older segments would not meet future requirements. During 1906, seven, 55 foot, interurban combines were delivered by Cincinnati Car Co. and given numbers #301-307. In addition, four deluxe, 61 foot, limited cars, also by Cincinnati, were added for the new, through Indianapolis service. These were #501-504 which had a smoking, parlor-buffet section, standard seat section and a spacious, enclosed observation rear end with "cozy corner" seats. Besides the regular crew, these cars carried a porter and steward. They were given individual names, derived from the work of Sir Walter Scott, to make them more distinctive (Kenilworth, Talisman, Ivanhoe and Woodstock).

In 1909, four more standard interurban cars were added as #308-311. They were very similar to the other Cincinnati built 300's, but rode on Curtis instead of Baldwin trucks. During the subsequent years all of these cars received some rebuilding and minor modifications at the Huntington Shops with #303 considerably rebuilt following the Kingsland wreck.

The arrival of the new 300's meant some changes for the Southwestern's 300's. These earlier combines were rebuilt to coaches and converted to passenger trailers #81-85. The 205's and the 84-85 disappeared from the records at an early date. One of the 205's was severely damaged at the Boyd Park barn. Trailer #81 was on the property, but off its trucks in 1920, while #82 and #83 survived until the middle thirties.

At this point the metamorphis of some of these missing cars begins to take shape with all, or parts of them appearing in a number of "new" cars. The first of these was #800, the "Lawton", named for Fort Wayne's Spanish American War hero, General Henry F. Lawton who was killed in the Phillipines. From all descriptions, the Lawton, built at the Huntington shops in 1906, was one of the missing cars specially rebuilt for the top brass to use on inspection trips and for chartered parties. It was nicely fitted out with lounge chairs, office facilities, a kitchen for light meals and big glass ends. After about fifteen years of this service it was assigned to the paymaster as pay car for the entire system. No doubt it became the most popular car on the line. Even in later years it was trundled from Spy Run to Baker St. to pay local employees assigned to those barns. Apparantly it was scrapped about 1930 and no photo seems to exist of one of the best employee remembered cars.

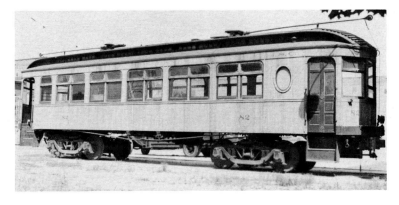

Trailer #82, at Spy Run Shops in 1936, was formerly a Southwestern line car.

Between 1910 and 1913 three, large, composite wood and steel, 61 foot interurban cars were built at Huntington. The #320 and #321 were similar, but not alike although both were built in 1910. This would seem to indicate that one each of the old #205 and first 300 class were taken in hand and totally reconstructed, although so much new construction was involved it would be difficult to tell which was built from what. In 1913 the very sturdy looking and heavier #322 appeared and it may have had parts from an earlier car but appears to be mostly new construction.

Trucks, controls, and frames were re-used in work equipment. Some of the line cars and M. of W. equipment built during this period bears a resemblence to, or have equipment from, the missing cars. This was typical of the resourcefullness of all electric railways whether large or small.

A major program was undertaken during 1920-21 in which all the interurban cars were considerably rebuilt and partially standardized. Those with proper control for multiple unit operations were equipped for two car train service. Front and rear draw bars were added to all the 300's not already having them, except #302 and #303 which had them only on the rear end, and m.u. connectors added. The 500's were re-numbered to the 350 series and rear end draw bars added. The observation section was removed with vestibule and seating arranged to conform with the 300's.

The fast m.u. cars were put on the through runs while the others ran singly or dragged trailers on local runs. The m.u. cars had the ability to get-up-and-go, were used for special movements, and displaced the 350's on the long limited runs.

When I. S. C. acquired the Fort Wayne and Northwestern and assumed operating control of the Lima line, new cars became a must. Both of these lines had little left that was servicable for passenger service with the cars of the Lima line hardly fit to be on wheels.

Ten, medium-weight, steel, two-man cars were delivered by St. Louis Car Co. and placed in service on these lines. The Northern Division received four, numbered 323-326 with the balance assigned to the Fort Wayne - Lima R. R. as #90-95. These cars were carefully designed by I. S. C. engineers and, during 1927, the 323-326 were easily turned end-for-end and converted to one-man cars. The #324 was proudly displayed at the A. E. R. A. (American Electric Railway Association) convention in Cleveland that year. In those days it was a simple matter to run the car from Fort Wayne to Cleveland via the connecting Ohio traction lines.

The swing to steel cars was begun to eliminate the wooden cars and their attendant hazards. The switch was still in the planning stages when the Roanoke accident occurred totally destroying the #306 and wrecking #322 so badly that it was retired from passenger service and rebuilt to a freight motor. In 1925, the 351 tangled with Union Traction's all steel 409, south of Peru, and was totally destroyed.

The Fort Wayne - Decatur line, although independent, had been under the supervision of the Ft. W. & N. I. and I. S. C. since 1916. They had purchased three, medium-weight, steel cars (101-103) to replace the old wooden cars. These steel cars were similar to the 323 series and the #103 was experimentally rebuilt to resemble the newer one-manned cars. It emerged a totally changed car as number #327. The other two were not rebuilt and came into the I. S. C. stable following the junking of the Decatur line. They were little used, as they required a two-man crew, and spent most of their remaining years stored at the Kendallville barn. Both were leased to Indiana Railroad but remained in storage until scrapped in 1936.

On the opposite page, the company built 320 series interurbans. Top: The 320 built in 1910. Middle: The 321, also built in 1910. Bottom: Last in the series, the 322, built in 1913.

I. S. C. #324, a Northern Division interurban lightweight, at the Spy Run Avenue yards, in 1923.

End-for-end, one man for two, the 324 sits on proud display at the Cleveland A. E. R. A. convention of 1927. The car went to Cleveland via the connecting interurban lines.

I. S. C. #327, at the end of the Broadway line, was rebuilt in 1927 from Ft. Wayne-Decatur #103. This was a complete re-design rebuilding job to match the car with the 323's.

St. Louis Car Company's advance photos of the new, heavy steel cars in 1926. The seven cars were among the best and heaviest built for any interurban.

The 90's were not converted to one-man cars and became surplus in 1933 when the Lima line folded. Probably due to their lower mileage, stored servicable for some time, and since Indiana Railroad was operating #323-326, they were the better buy for Oklahoma Railways who acquired part of them.

In continuing the modernization and to upgrade the mainline service, an order was placed in 1926, for seven, steel interurban cars. These cars were the ultimate in the construction of heavy, deluxe, pure interurban cars. Five of these, fast and well-powered cars, were combines and the other two, special Parlor-Buffet cars. Their arrival meant that only a few of the older, but well maintained, wooden cars were needed in service.

The "Anthony Wayne" and "Little Turtle" were especially distinctive in the parlor car field. They were not trailers tagging along, but powered and capable of operation by themselves. Normal operation called for them to be coupled to one of the new combines and operated in multiple unit. These trains were the new version of the "Wabash Valley Flyer" operating to Indianapolis, via Peru, on a four hour schedule for the 135 mile run. This train, on the northbound run, was joined at Peru with the "Indiana Flyer" from Lafayette and run jointly to Fort Wayne. Other named runs were the "University Limited", and "Second City Limited". Most of these were known as "County Seat" trains making only the major stops. Similar service was maintained by Union Traction, via Bluffton, with the best known of these trains the "Hoosierland".

These fancy services were far from lucrative, maintained only for prestige, with the bread and butter business being the local customers and their produce. Indiana Railroad quit these plush runs and returned the parlor cars to I. S. C. Their heavy weight and attendant power consumption, plus a complicated electrical system made them un-economical to operate and impractical for conversion to one-man cars.

Two of the combines were one-manned by Indiana Railroad and had the dubious honor of being the first such cars retired by them. The other three were rebuilt with a Railway Post Office section and operated until 1941. These three were sold to the South Shore Line where

Fort Wayne - Decatur #102 was stored at Kendallville for years. It was used for experimental paint schemes and, although leased to Indiana R. R., was never used in passenger service.

Top: Marion & Bluffton's #340 was kept as a spare car. Middle: #325 being dismantled at Spy Run in 1938. Bottom: Oklahoma Rys. #223, in 1947, at Norman, Oklahoma. The car was formerly a F. W. - L. 90 series car.

I. R. R. #376 (above) stored in the South Shore yards after being sold, by I. S. C., along with 375 and 377. Superb line car (below) #1100 was built from 376, by the South Shore in 1947.

two are now express trailers and the other, one of the finest line cars in the world.

When Indiana Railroad took over the Western (Lafayette) and Southern (Bluffton) divisions a number of I. S. C. cars were leased to them. Most of the freight motors, some of the work equipment and most of the newer passenger cars were in this group, including #375-379, #390-391, #101-102 and #201-202. Used, but apparantly not leased, were #323-327 which continued to run on the Northern Division. The #327 was retired first and not repainted for Indiana Railroad. The old wooden cars were stored and later scrapped at the McKinley Avenue yards.[6]

The Marion and Bluffton company placed cars #201-202 in service just before the I. S. C. acquired it. These McGuire-Cummings built light-weights were the first one-man interurban cars on the system. They were continued in use by Indiana Railroad although not re-lettered, until the line was torn up in 1931. Brought back to Fort Wayne, the pair were stored at Spy Run. They were not suitable for use elsewhere and eventually scrapped along with the rest of the Marion and Bluffton equipment.

The freight and service fleet was large, all inclusive and a definite hodge-podge. Some of it was bought new but the bulk was company built and often rebuilt. Many of the old wooden cars were rebuilt into freight and service equipment. I. S. C.'s engineers developed a fairly standard and distinctive design for the equipment built at Spy Run. Many specialty car types were needed for the far flung interurban system and its four small city operations. One large

Top: City car #125 freshly rebuilt to plow #1, sits outside the Chestnut barn entrance as a cigar store indian looks on.
Bottom: The 21, in one of its several forms, at work on Wells Street in 1923.

Spy Run yard with the brand new 28 and flat car 1102. The 28, later #828, was formerly F. W. & N. W. #7 and was classed as the "Tool and Equipment" car by I. S. C.

The new Fort Wayne, Commerce Drive, freight terminal in February 1927. I. S. C. #50 (the only known picture of this short lived car) later 850, and Union Traction's #704 plus numerous freight trailers. At least four different types of traction freight car construction can be seen.

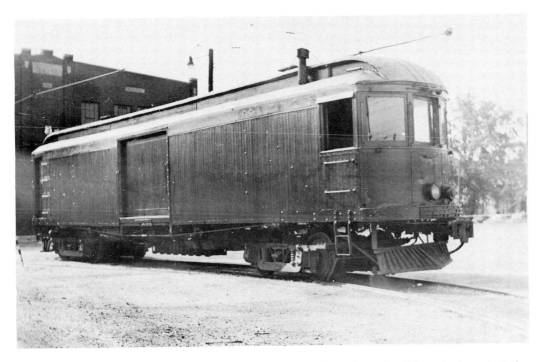

No name and no number distinguished the 848 in Indiana & Michigan Electric Co. service. Only one track remains in the old car yards which were used for the bus fleet.

Fort Wayne - Lima R.R. freight motor #35 at the freight terminal in the late twenties. This car was rebuilt for freight service from an old Ohio Electric passenger car.

Fort Wayne & Wabash Valley's 250, used on the Battleground line at the Ferry Street car barn in Lafayette, Indiana.

Line car #41, about 1906, at Peru. The car, originally a 250 series city car, was rebuilt in 1906. Later it was modified to a different style becoming #25 and #825.

line car and several smaller service cars were permanently assigned to each city to serve the local and immediate interurban lines. The company had more than fifty such cars and over seventy five freight cars. Some of these cars were leased to Indiana Railroad and others scrapped soon after 1931 as useless. The rest eventually suffered the same fate.

A few cars continued in service in Fort Wayne and vicinity. These included snow plows, sweepers, sprinklers, wreck and sand cars. All of these were scrapped by 1947.

Two interurban motors outlasted everything in Fort Wayne. Numbers #817 and #848 continued in service on the Northern Division remains. Until 1952, #817 continued to switch cars on Spy Run Avenue and East State Boulevard.

Equipment Assignments - The small city lines.

The heavy interurban equipment, both freight and passenger, might be found anywhere on the system but certain city car classes or types held fairly fixed assignments. The four small city lines were strung out along the long Fort Wayne - Lafayette interurban route. This direct connection allowed cars to be freely switched from one to another as needed. Baker Street and later Spy Run became the "home base" for these cars whenever rebuilding or other modifications were necessary as it was more economical to maintain only one well equipped shop. Light running or emergency repairs were made at the Boyd Park, Logansport or Lafayette barns. The transfer of cars was usually made at night and the running of a low wheeled, single truck car over a 120 mile line must have been quite a trip.

The following lists are based on equipment assignments as of January 1, 1918 when each line was in its heyday and probably near the peak of its assignments.[7] Usually these lesser properties received older cars displaced from Fort Wayne. Lafayette originally had a surplus of cars, kept for peak operations at the far end of the line, which were normally housed at the Kossuth Street Barns. This barn and the surplus burned May 20, 1915 with neither replaced.[8]

Lafayette, in 1918, had ten of the #140-56 class which were normally kept there and had been sent out in the early 1900's to replace the original closed cars. The seven Brill nearsides, #221-227, were built for Lafayette use and remained there until 1920. Two of the double truck 250's were assigned to the Battleground line and the two fifteen bench opens, #370-371, were based at the Ninth Street barn. Only four, one power and three trail, eight bench opens were used on the city lines. One snow sweeper and one work car rounded out the listing. A heavy line car was based in Lafayette for use on the city routes and interurban line.

Logansport, at the same date, had nine closed cars for use. Three came from the #109-119 group, two from the #140-156 group and the remaining four seem to have been #170-173. Ten motorized open cars were broken down as follows – four eight bench, one nine bench, and five ten bench. A snow sweeper and work car completed the collection. Again, another heavy line car was based in the area for the city and interurban lines.

Wabash and Peru had two cars each. The Wabash cars were from the #140-156 group whereas Peru appears to have had #174-175. These cars usually sat outside as there was no barn in either city. The interurban cars handled the snow plowing job in both cities.

These assignments, which were fairly permanent for several years, were somewhat changed after 1920, when many new cars arrived in Fort Wayne releasing some of the older cars for use elsewhere. Most of the old cars came back to Fort Wayne and eventually junked.

Logansport was modernized with new cars, #290-299, in an attempt to attract riders and improve service. Peru and Wabash received a succession of cars from the #176-201 group and later the #202-220 class. From 1932 until 1934, when the Peru line was the sole survivor, the new single truckers from the #290-299 group were used.

Top: Work motor 820 at the Wabash, Indiana station on August 3, 1926. The old number 20 can still be seen. Middle: Line motor 829, built from Ft. Wayne - Decatur 110, at the Peru passenger station on August 3, 1936. Bottom: Freight motor 846, one of the last built by I. S. C., at Wabash, Indiana.

ROLLING STOCK

(Based On 1920 Inventory)

No.	Builder	Year Built	Truck	Motor	Controls	Notes
109	J. M. Jones Co.	1902	Peckham	2-GE1000	2-K10	Double end, single truck deck roof cars
112	J. M. Jones Co.	1902	Peckham	2-GE1000	2-K10	built for Ft. Wayne Traction. The origi-
113	J. M. Jones Co.	1902	Peckham	2-GE67	2-K10	nal number built is unknown. All out of
117	J. M. Jones Co.	1902	Peckham	2-GE67	2-K10	service by 1923.
119	J. M. Jones Co.	1902	Peckham	2-GE67	2-K10	
133	J. M. Jones Co.	1902	Peckham	2-GE67	2-K10	
121-131	Ft. W. Traction	1902 1903	Peckham	2-GE1000	2-K10	Homebuilt, double end, single truck, deck roof cars. Out of service 1923. No. 125 became #1.
140-156	Cincinnati and Barney & Smith	1904	Curtis	2-GE216	2-K36 Or 2-K10	Deck roof cars, single truck, by both builders with numbers intermingled. Curtis truck added. Out in 1927.
169	St. Louis	1905	Curtis	2-GE216	2-K36	Removed from service 1922.
170-173	Cincinnati	1907	Peckham	2-GE216	2-K10	170-175 Deck roof, single truck cars. Semi-convertible type. 170-173 out in
174	Cincinnati	1907	Peckham	2-GE216	2-K36	1930. 174-175 in 1924.
175	Cincinnati	1907	Peckham	2-GE80	2-K10	
176-201	Cincinnati	1909	Curtis	2-GE80	2-K10	Deck roof, single truck, cars semi-convertible type. Last one out in 1934.
202-220	Cincinnati	1913	Curtis	2-GE216	2-K35	Arch roof, single truck, P.A.Y.E. Nearside cars. Originally single end only. 209 lasted until 1937.
221-227	J. G. Brill	1913	Brill-21E	2-GE216	1-K36	Nearside, P.A.Y.E. cars. All but 225 out in 1922. 225 made double end out 1926.
240-249	St. Louis	1917	Baldwin	4-WH506	2-K12A	Two man, rear entrance cars 249 had St. Louis trucks. Rebuilt to 500-509, 1922-23.
250	American	1901	Peckham	4-GE67	2-K6	Double truck, suburban, deck roof cars
251	American	1901	Peckham	4-GE67	4-K6	from Wabash River Traction 10-11 and
252	American	1901	McGuire	4-GE1000	2-K6	14-17. Nos. 250, 252, 253 out early,
253	American	1901	McGuire	4-GE1000	2-K6	rest in 1924.
254	American	1901	Peckham	4-GE67	2-K6	250-251 41'3", Curved sides
255	American	1901	McGuire	4-GE1000	2-K6	253-255 39'6", Stright sides
275-299	St. Louis	1918	St. L. 113	2 GE258	2-K63B	Arch roof single truck cars, 291-299 built with Curtis truck. Out in 1940.
370-371	American	1901	McGuire	4-GE67	1-K6	15 bench opens. Retired in 1924.
400-434	St. Louis	1919	St. L. 113	2-GE258	2-K36BR	Arch roof city cars. 400 became sand car. Out 1940.
435-449	St. Louis	1922	St. L. 113	2-GE258	2-K63BR	Same as 400-434.
500-509	St. Louis	1917	Baldwin	4-WH506	2-K35	Rebuilt from 240-249. 508 had upper sash covered.
510-524	St. Louis	1923	St. Louis	2-GE264A	2-K35J	Double truck, arch roof city cars. 543 last car in Ft. Wayne. Several cars sold to other properties. 523 burned
525-539	St. Louis	1924	St. Louis	2-GE264A	2-K35J	in 1930.

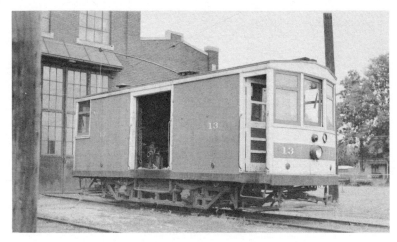

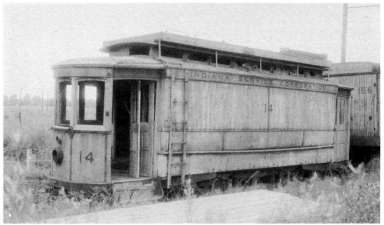

Top: Work car 13 reflects the good maintainance of I. S. C.'s active cars. Middle: Old sand car 14 awaits scrapping at the McKinley yard in 1937. Bottom: Coke car 130 was the shell of an old passenger car of Northwestern or Decatur lineage.

ROLLING STOCK

No.	Builder	Year Built	Truck	Motor	Controls	Notes
540-544	St. Louis	1925	St. Louis	2-GE264A	2-K35J	

Interurban Passenger Cars (wooden)

No.	Builder	Year Built	Truck	Motor	Controls	Notes
81-85	John Stephenson Company	1901	Peckham			Trailers, ex F.W.&S.W. 301-305 Only 81-83 listed 1920. 82-83 changed to Baldwin trucks.
205-208	Jackson & Sharp	1902	Peckham			Little known about these Southwestern cars.
301	Cincinnati	1906	Baldwin	4-GE205	1-L4	55 foot interurban combines. Remodeled several times 303 rebuilt after the Kingsland wreck. 302, 304, 305, 306, 307 made M. U. 306 destroyed at Roanoke May 19, 1924.
302	Cincinnati	1906	Baldwin	4-GE205	1-HL	
303	Cincinnati	1906	Baldwin	4-GE205	1-HL	
304	Cincinnati	1906	Baldwin	4-WH121	1-HL	
305	Cincinnati	1906	Baldwin	4-WH121	1-HL	
306	Cincinnati	1906	Baldwin	4-WH121	1-HL	
307	Cincinnati	1906	Baldwin	4-WH121	1-HL	
308-311	Cincinnati	1909	Curtis	4-GE205	1-L4	Like 301-307. 301-311 moderized in 1922-23.
320	Ft. W. & W. V.	1910	Baldwin	4-WH121	1-H6	Composite wood-steel interurban combine 63' long.
321	Ft. W. & W. V.	1910	Baldwin	4-WH121	Type M	Composite wood-steel interurban combine 63' long.
322	Ft. W. & N. I.	1913	Baldwin	4-WH303	1-HL	Composite wood-steel interurban combine 63' long. Wrecked at Roanoke May 19, 1924. Rebuilt as 853.
351-354	Cincinnati	1906	Baldwin	4-WH121	1-L4	Ex 501-504. Deluxe limited combines, 61' 6" long. Had two large rear windows. Rebuilt 1922. 351 wrecked June 3, 1925.
800	Ft. W. & W. V.	1906	Peckham 26	4-GE67	1-K35	"Lawton", Official car.

Interurban Passenger Cars (Steel)

No.	Builder	Year Built	Truck	Motor	Controls	Notes
323-326	St. Louis	1923	Commonwealth	4-GE275	1-K35	Ten cars built identical four used on I.S.C. and six on F.W.-L. line. I.S.C.'s made one man 1927, junked 1937
90-95	St. Louis	1923	Commonwealth	4-GE275	1-K35	F.W.-L. cars sold to Oklahoma Railways and junked 1946.
327	St. Louis	1927	Commonwealth	4-GE275	1-K35	Rebuilt 1927 from Ft. W.-Decatur 103, built 1916.
101-102	St. Louis	1916	Baldwin 73	4-GE	1-K35	Ex F.W.&D. Tr. Co. 101-102. Leased to I.R.R. Out 1936.
201-202	Cimmings C.&C.	1925	Cummings	4-GE	1-?	Ex Marion & Bluffton one man lightweights. Leased to I.R.R. Out of service in 1931. Scrapped soon after.
375-379	St. Louis	1926	Baldwin	4-WH333	W-HL	Steel interurban combines. Wt. 101,000 lbs. leased to I.R.R. 378-379 scrapped in 1938. 375-377 sold to C.S.S.&S.B., now 1100, 503-4
390-391	St. Louis	1926	Baldwin	2-WH333	W-HL	Deluxe parlor cars, 390 "Little Turtle", 391 "Anthony Wayne". Leased to I.R.R. scrapped 1937.

Top: Sand car 400 was used until 1940. Note the timken truck on the flat car. Middle: Snow sweeper #4 built in 1895. Bottom: Snow sweeper #7, built by the company in 1915 as nearly identical to #4. All the above photographed in 1937.

ROLLING STOCK

No.	Builder	Year Built	Truck	Motor	Controls	Notes
			Work and Line Equipment			
1	Ft. W. & N.I.	1918	Curtis	2-GE216	2-K35	Wing snow plow, from 125.
2	McGuire - Cum.	1895	McGuire	2-GE1000	3-K10	#2 sold to Lafyette St. Rys.
3	McGuire - Cum.	1895	McGuire	2-GE1000	3-K10	2-7 snow sweepers
4	McGuire - Cum.	1895	McGuire	2-GE1000	3-K10	1-GE800 motor for broom operation
5	McGuire - Cum.	1905	McGuire	2-GE1000	3-K10	
7	Ft. W. & N.I.	1915	McGuire	2-GE1000	3-K10	
8	Company	—	Dorner	2-GE52	2-K10	Sand car, out 1937
10	I. S. C.	1921	Curtis	Trailer		Single truck, ex 1029 Trash car
11	Ft. W. & N.I.	?	Peckham	2-GE800	1-K2	Work car
13	Company	1920	Peckham	2-Loraine	2-K10	Wreck car. Curtis truck 1924.
14	J. M. Jones	?	Peckham	2-GE1000	2-K10	Sand car, Curtis truck 1924
15	McGuire - Cum.	1909	Pedestal	2-?	2-?	3000 Gal. sprinkler
16	Elec. Ry. Imp. Co.	1908	trail			Bonding car
17	J. M. Jones	—	Peckham	2-GE1000	2-K10	Work car, junked 1925
19	Company	—	Curtis			Work car
817	I. S. C.	1925	Baldwin	4-GE205	2-HL	Ex 17 Switch motor from F.W.&N.W. 8 built in 1906. Last car in Ft. Wayne.
818	I. S. C.	1925	Baldwin	4-GE205B	2-HL	Ex 18, built from F.W.&N.W. 5 Center cab work motor to I.R.R. 792
820	Ft. W. & N.I.	1912	Baldwin	4-WH121	2-L4	Ex 20 work mtr. to I.R.R. 793
821	Company	1912	Peckham	4-WH85	1-L4	Ex 21, to I.R.R. 794, built with Brill trucks. Like 818
822	I. S. C.	1921	Baldwin	4-?	2-?	Ex 819 M. of W. car to I.R.R. 795
823	Ft. W. & N.I.	—	Peckham	2-GE101	1-L4	Ex 42, Line Motor, reel in the rear.
824	Ft. W. & N.I.	—	Peckham	2-GE201	2-K6	Ex 43, Line Motor
825	Ft. W. & N.I.	1910	Peckham 26	2-GE201	2-K6	Ex 25, ex 41 Line car. From 250 series car
826	Ft. W. & N.I.	1910	Baldzin	4-GE216	2-K6	Ex 26, ex 40. As 825 rebuilt in 1939 with new trucks from an 80 class trailer (note 823-6, all similar)
827	I. S. C.	1924	Peckham	4-GE214	2-K34	Line car, ex F. W. & N. W. #1
828	I. S. C.	1924	Baldwin	4-GE214	2-K34	Tool & Equipment car, from F. W. & N.W. # 7
829	I. S. C.	1929	Baldwin	4-WH307	1-K6a	Line motor from salvage of Ft.W.-D.#110
845	I. S. C.	1930	Baldwin	4-GE205	2-HL	From salvage of F.W.-L.40 to I.R.R.726
846	I. S. C.	1930	Baldwin	4-GE205	2-HL	From salvage of F.W.-L.42 to I.R.R.727
847	I. S. C.	1930	Curtis	4-GE205	1-L4	Ex 47, from F.W.-L.47 to I.R.R.728
848	I. S. C.	1926	Baldwin	4-GE205	2-HL	Ex 48, from F.W.&N.W.#3
849	I. S. C.	1926	Baldwin	4-?	1-L4	Ex pass. car burned before 1930
850	I. S. C.	1927	?	4-?	2-?	Ex 50, from passenger car
851	I. S. C.	1926	Peckham	4-?	2-HL	From F.W.&N.W. car, to wreck car, to I.R.R. 1153
852	Cincinnati	1905	Baldwin	4-WH85	2-L4	Ex 52, Frt. Motor to I.R.R. 729
853	I. S. C.	1924	Baldwin	4-GE205	2-HL	Ex 53, ex passenger 322, wrecked 2nd time at France siding on F.W.-L. line August 21, 1929. Rebuilt with parts from F.W.-L. 44 to I.R.R. 730
854-855	Cincinnati	1907	Baldwin	4-WH85	1-L4	Ex 54, 55. Freight motors to I.R.R. 731-732
856-857	Cincinnati	1910	Curtis	2-GE205	1-L4	Ex 56-57. Freight motors to I.R.R. 733-734
858-859	St. Louis	1917	Baldwin	4-WH85	1-HL	Ex 58-59. Freight motors to I.R.R. 735-736

Line motors 827 and 826 on their last assignment. The pair were used in the dismantling of the Bluffton line, early in 1941.

Crane #14 on the coal track behind the Spy Run power house in January 1916. The number was later deleted and the little crane continued in use until it was junked in 1962 after ten years of inactivity. This was the last rail equipment owned by I. & M. at Fort Wayne.

ROLLING STOCK

No.	Builder	Year Built	Truck	Motor	Controls	Notes
Portable Substations (Westinghouse Equipped)						
999	McGuire-Cum.	1906	Arch Bar trail			From Phila. Rapid Transit burned July 9, 1919.
1000	McGuire-Cum.	1910	Arch Bar trail			Bought new, all steel.
Freight Equipment						
130	Coke Car		Arch Bar trucks			Shell of a F. W. & N. W. or Ft. W. - D. wooden passenger car.
144-159	Box Freight		Arch Bar trucks			#144 from F.W.-D. #111, used as the freight house at Garrett until 1945. Several Builders in these
161-169	Box Freight		Arch Bar trucks			groups 144-159 and 161-169.
1001-1010	Gondolas		Haskel & Barker Co.			
1011-1017	Gravel Cars		Haffner - Thrall Co.			
1030-1033	Hopper Dump		Differential Steel Car Co.			
1034-1045	Side Dump		Differential Steel Car Co.			Capacity 80,000 lbs.
1046-1055	Side Dump		Differential Steel Car Co			Capacity 100,000 lbs.
1101-1110	Flat Cars		Company had no record of builder			
1118-1122	Flat Cars		Built by F.W. & N.W., Ft. W. & N.I. and I.S.C. (see also 1119)			
1123-1125	Flat Cars		I.S.C. built in 1938 from older cars. double truck			
1119	Boom Crane		Trailer with steam boom crane, retired in 1926.			
1140	Derrick Car		Double truck derrick car built by St. Louis in 1926.			
Maintenance Equipment						
	Thew Steam Shovel		Single Truck	1912		
	Weed Burner		Single Truck	1911		
	Tank for weed burner		Single Truck	1911		
	Rail Grinder		Single Truck	1911		
	Jaeger Cement Mixer		Single Truck	19??		Peckham truck
	Electric crane car		Single Truck	19??		Power House crane - formerly 14
	Portable Saw		Single Truck			Electrically powered circular saw.
Underlying Properties Equipment						

Fort Wayne & Northwestern Ry. Co. (Toledo & Chicago Interurban Ry. Co.)

No.	Builder	Year Built	Truck	Notes
1-2	Niles	1905	Peckham M. CB.	Double truck interurban coaches 45 feet long
3-4	Niles	1906	Peckham M. CB.	Double truck interurban combines 52 feet long
5-8	Niles	1906	Baldwin M. C. B.	Double truck interurban combines 52 feet long
50-51	Niles	1906	Peckham MC. B	Double truck freight motors 52 feet long
101		1906	Trailer	Freight trailer
?	Company	1905	Brill - 27	Work motor, used in construction.

All equipment originally powered by 3300 volt A. C., converted to D. C. in 1913

Fort Wayne - Decatur Tr. Co. (Fort Wayne & Springfield Ry. Co.)

No.	Builder	Year Built	Truck	Notes
1-3	Niles	1906	Baldwin	53' wooden passenger combines
50	Niles	1906	Peckham	44' Freight Motor
101	?	?	?	Portable Substation
111	?	?	?	Freight Trailer

This equipment used 6600 volt A. C. power with Bow Trolley collectors. Trolley poles used in Fort Wayne when running on 600 volt D. C.

The interior of the Kendallville barn in 1906 showing the rather temporary nature of what was expected to be a temporary structure on the Toledo & Chicago line. The picture illustrates the rugged construction of the heavy-duty Peckham MCB interurban truck. Car #5, in the background, rides on Baldwin trucks.

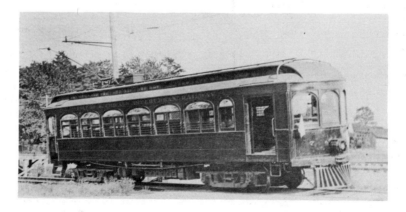

Toledo & Chicago #7, one of the Niles built 52 foot combines. The car is equipped for operation at 3300 volts A.C. and is running under caternary overhead wire. White flags would indicate this was an "extra" and possibly out for a record picture in 1906.

ROLLING STOCK

No.	Builder	Year Built	Truck	Motor	Controls	Notes
101-103	St. Louis	1917	Baldwin 73			Single end steel combines. Became 101, 102, 327 on I. S. C.
110	St. Louis	1917	Baldwin 73			Express motor

Fort Wayne, Van Wert & Lima Tr. Co.

No.	Builder	Year Built	Truck	Motor	Controls	Notes
1-10	Jewett	1905	Taylor			Turned over to Ohio Electric under lease agreements.
101-102	Cincinnati	1906	Baldwin			Limited cars similar to Ft. W. & W. V. 500 series. Purchased by Lima - Toledo.

Note:
Cars 1-10 became Ohio Electric 79-87 and were considerably rebuilt. Car 82 wrecked March 27, 1910. Known cars returned to the company were 79, 80, 81. Also O. E. cars 77 and 295-297 became 47, 48
All these cars were rebuilt into freight and service cars. See page 147 for additional notes

Marion & Bluffton Traction Co. (Marion, Bluffton & Eastern Tr. Co.)

No.	Builder	Year Built	Truck	Motor	Controls	Notes
325	Niles	1906	Taylor	4-WH	K14	45' combines, wt. 62,400 lbs.
330	Niles	1906	Taylor	4-WH	K14	
335	Niles	1906	Taylor	4-WH	K14	
340	Niles	1906	Taylor	4-WH	K14	
345	Niles	1906	Taylor	4-WH	K14	
350	Cincinnati	1908				Suburban type cars, double trucks. 350 destroyed by 330 July 7, 1912.
355	Cincinnati	1910				Express motor of M. B. & E.
264	Niles	1906	Taylor	4-WH		Express motor, This was probably the jointly operated motor belonging to B. G. & C.
278	Cincinnati	1906	Taylor	4-WH		
150	Express Trailer					
201-202	Cummings	1925	Cummings	4-GE		One man lightweights

Bluffton, Geneva & Celina Traction Co.

Controled by the M. B. & E. and in joint operation. Cars of both companies were used on the B. G. & C. The company owned one freight motor probably the 278 and one trailer freight car for hauling milk.

No.	Builder	Year Built	Truck	Motor	Controls	Notes
400	Jewett	1909	Taylor			53'8'' combine sold to Union Traction as 416 in 1917

M. B. & E. #330, in service for I. S. C. at VanBuren, Indiana in 1927. These old wooden cars were used as spares for the 200 class lightweights purchased in 1925.

Dapper Dan, complete with straw sailor, gladstone bag and umbrella, stands on the steps of a Toledo & Chicago car, about 1908. The iron straps on the pole shows that the heavy overhead had caused it to split.

ROLLING STOCK

No.	Builder	Year Built	Truck	Motor	Controls	Notes
Fort Wayne - Lima R. R. Co.						
Passenger Cars						
90- 95	St. Louis	1923	Commonwealth	4-GE275	1-K35	Semi-lightweight steel cars in part. Never one manned sold to Oklahoma Rys.
Freight and Service						
31	I. S. C.			4-	2-	Line Car.
32	I. S. C.		Baldwin			32, 33, 35 Double end freight motor, from old passenger cars, 34 Single end,
33	I. S. C.		Baldwin			freight motor. All similar except 32
34	I. S. C.		Baldwin		1-	which had an arch roof instead of rail-
35	I. S. C.		Baldwin		2	road roof. The Co. also owned one work car and sixteen box cars.

FORT WAYNE CITY BUSES

Nos.	Builder	Date	Capacity	Notes
30- 33	F.W. & N. I. Studebaker	1917	16	Homebuilt bodies on truck chasis.
100- 104	International	1925	21	Intercity buses
110- 112	International	1926	29	Intercity buses
120- 121	International	1925	36	Traded to Hammond, Ind. for three A. C. F. buses.
200- 205	Fageol	1923-24	36	Intercitys. Came to I. S. C. from Golden Faun Bus-lines in 1925.
230	Fageol		31	
300- 302	White	?	34	Second hand, used in Logansport until 1931.
400- 407	Studebaker	1923	9	Small, city buses. 406-407 were somewhat larger. Probably seating 13.
421- 423	Studebaker	1925	16	Different style and larger than 400-407.
500- 502	Fargo	1931	25	Bought for use in Wabash. Used in Fort Wayne on W. Jeff. and W. State lines.
525	Reo	1922	21	Old type acquired by I. S. C.
600- 602	Yellow Coach	1929	29	City type buses for Fort Wayne.
1-7	A. C. F.	1939	26	Transit type city bus.
8-9	Ford	1940	26	Transit type city bus.
10- 11	A. C. F.	1939	26	Transit type city bus, 2nd hand.
455- 458	A. C. F.		31	2nd hand from Hammond, Indiana in 1928.

The present motor bus fleet (1963) is in a state of change, but is comprised of Twin Coach propane and gasoline powered motor buses and G. M. C. diesel buses. Some of the 1947-48 model 38-S and 41-S Twins are still in use.

When the trolley coach operation ended, the company had an immediate need for sixty buses. This was solved through the acquisition of 29 Twins from Buffalo, N. Y., and 30 Twins from Detroit, Michigan, all similar to those already is use. In 1961 and 1962 a number of used, late model, G. M. C. diesels were purchased and placed in service for comparison of operating costs. Inter-city diesel buses were also acquired for charter service.

More changes can be expected as the older buses are replaced with newer ones. The present fleet consists of 12 G. M. C. diesel buses, 41 Twins operating on propane, and 34 Twins operating on gasoline, for a total of 87 city type buses.

Portable sub-station #1000 parked on the spur track in the middle of Raymond Street near the Harvester loop at the end of the Pontiac line.

Toledo & Chicago's home-built, work motor with a ballast train in 1905. Construction methods were rather crude on many of the smaller interurban lines.

CHAPTER 12

||||||||||||||||||||||||||||||||||||||||||||||||||||||||||||||||||||||||||||||||||||||||||||||||||||||||||||||||||||||||||||||||||||||||||||||||||||||||||||||||||||||||||||||||||||||||||||||

Statistics

||||||||||||||||||||||||||||||||||||||||||||||||||||||||||||||||||||||||||||||||||||||||||||||||||||||||||||||||||||||||||||||||||||||||||||||||||||||||||||||||||||||||||||||||||||||||||||||

With the exception of the year 1919 accurate figures are available for the street and interurban railway lines from 1914 through 1947 when Indiana Service Corporation was disolved. Car Miles and Passengers Carried are the more complete as the breakdown for all divisions is available for the years mentioned. Operating Revenues, Expenses and Income are somewhat less complete as only overall total Operating Expenses are available for 1914 through 1917, although we do have these figures complete from 1918.[1]

The figures largely tell their own story and present some interesting sidelight information not visible in the general history of the company. For instance a check of the figures will show that the four small city properties were far from profitable ventures. The Logansport operations were losing money in 1918 when new cars were placed in service. The improvement was a decided success as the number of passengers increased by 1,300,000 between 1918 and 1920 which put the operation back in the profit column. By the late twenties it was again in the red with small losses sufficient enough to bring the abandonment proceedings in 1932 when the property would have been separated by the end of the connecting interurbans.

The Fort Wayne City Lines show an overall consistent profit picture with the exception of 1932, 1938 and 1940. Riding took a four and a half million drop in 1930. Passenger riding reached an all time peak in 1944 although profits never surpassed the 1923 high. Increased expenses, largely wages, were responsible for this.

The interurban lines present a different picture as net losses begin to appear in 1925 at the peak of the rehabilitation program and never show a profit again. These figures are deceptive and confusing after 1930 when the western and southern lines went to Indiana Railroad operation. The Northern Division continued to be run by I. S. C. through Indiana Railroad until 1937 producing continued losses. From 1937 until 1945 freight service continued on the Fort Wayne - Garrett portion of the line and in the city, once again producing a small net profit. These operations were confined to switching cars in Fort Wayne from 1945 to 1952.

The Fort Wayne statistics include bus and street car operations together. From 1940 through 1945 about 50 per cent of the revenues were produced by buses and from 1945 until 1947, when street cars were removed from service, approximately 90 per cent of the operation was by buses.

INDIANA SERVICE CORPORATION

OPERATING REVENUES, OPERATING EXPENSES AND OPERATING INCOME
STREET AND INTERURBAN RAILWAY LINES
YEARS 1914 TO 1919, INCL.

	1914	1915	1916	1917	1918	1919
OPERATING REVENUES						
Fort Wayne - City Lines	501,680	383,004	464,511	566,675	573,318	730,808
Wabash - City Lines	18,884	18,336	20,201	19,505	17,772	21,499
Peru - City Lines	18,385	11,634	10,067	9,858	14,304	13,942
Logansport - City Lines	78,439	69,785	54,494	63,793	65,733	113,303
Lafayette - City Lines	151,803	155,744	157,510	154,849	167,098	196,407
Interurban Lines	584,517	562,886	599,434	633,113	657,046	834,170
Total Operating Revenues	1,353,708	1,201,389	1,300,217	1,447,793	1,495,272	1,910,132
OPERATING EXPENSES						
Fort Wayne - City Lines	—	—	—	—	553,271	649,481
Wabash - City Lines	—	—	—	—	26,392	22,944
Peru - City Lines	—	—	—	—	25,641	23,166
Logansport - City Lines	—	—	—	—	97,909	97,308
Lafayette - City Lines	—	—	—	—	199,127	231,576
Interurban Lines	—	—	—	—	463,941	675,911
Total Operating Expenses	1,107,969	1,067,745	1,130,623	1,130,217	1,366,281	1,700,389
NET OPERATING INCOME						
Fort Wayne - City Lines	—	—	—	—	20,047	81,327
Wabash - City Lines	—	—	—	—	(8,620)	(1,444)
Peru - City Lines	—	—	—	—	(11,337)	(9,223)
Logansport - City Lines	—	—	—	—	(32,176)	15,994
Lafayette - City Lines	—	—	—	—	(32,028)	(35,169)
Interurban Lines	—	—	—	—	193,105	158,258
Total Net Operating Income	245,739	133,644	169,594	87,567	128,991	209,742

( ) Loss

INDIANA SERVICE CORPORATION

OPERATING REVENUES, OPERATING EXPENSES AND OPERATING INCOME
STREET AND INTERURBAN RAILWAY LINES
YEARS 1920 TO 1926, INCL.

	1920	1921	1922	1923	1924	1925	1926
OPERATING REVENUES							
Fort Wayne - City Lines	884,198	914,463	981,971	1,134,497	1,164,883	1,175,617	1,181,316
Wabash - City Lines	24,298	20,310	19,944	20,219	20,353	17,113	15,767
Peru - City Lines	21,973	17,065	15,655	16,094	24,640	23,153	22,700
Logansport - City Lines	137,456	126,414	120,173	124,063	115,497	107,301	101,227
Lafayette - City Lines	65,506	—	—	—	—	—	—
Interurban Lines	930,405	886,570	888,326	977,770	930,043	1,012,086	1,175,187
Total Operating Revenues	2,063,836	1,964,822	2,026,069	2,272,643	2,255,416	2,335,270	2,496,197
OPERATING EXPENSES							
Fort Wayne - City Lines	662,013	680,078	680,198	744,089	830,869	839,522	808,502
Wabash - City Lines	21,582	24,240	21,742	21,075	28,590	24,937	25,077
Peru - City Lines	19,144	19,587	17,857	17,920	26,557	26,020	27,061
Logansport - City Lines	96,617	106,112	95,568	93,378	112,548	104,360	97,584
Lafayette - City Lines	68,577	—	—	—	—	—	—
Interurban Lines	762,071	777,061	726,682	752,915	929,170	1,054,623	1,264,784
Total Operating Expenses	1,630,004	1,607,078	1,542,047	1,629,377	1,927,734	2,049,462	2,223,008
NET OPERATING INCOME							
Fort Wayne - City Lines	222,185	234,385	301,773	390,408	334,014	336,095	372,814
Wabash - City Lines	2,716	(3,930)	(1,798)	(856)	(8,237)	(7,824)	(9,310)
Peru - City Lines	2,829	(2,522)	(2,202)	(1,826)	(1,917)	(2,867)	(4,361)
Logansport - City Lines	40,839	20,302	24,605	30,685	2,950	2,941	3,643
Lafayette - City Lines	(3,071)	—	—	—	—	—	—
Interurban Lines	168,334	109,509	161.644	224,855	872	(42,537)	(89,597)
Total Net Operating Income	433,832	357,744	484,022	643.266	327,682	285,808	273,189

( ) Loss

INDIANA SERVICE CORPORATION

OPERATING REVENUES, OPERATING EXPENSES AND OPERATING INCOME
STREET AND INTERURBAN RAILWAY LINES
YEARS 1927 TO 1933, INCL.

	1927	1928	1929	1930	1931	1932	1933
OPERATING REVENUES							
Fort Wayne - City Lines	1,136,986	1,111,080	1,210,567	1,098,595	897,261	635,631	571,636
Wabash - City Lines	15,050	15,223	14,292	9,310	5,112	—	—
Peru - City Lines	22,558	26,091	25,414	19,161	13,482	10,474	7,140
Logansport - City Lines	90,374	83,867	84,481	68,541	50,462	18,587	—
Lafayette - City Lines	—	—	—	—	--	—	—
Interurban Lines	1,132,757	1,038,395	1,091,946	778,759	581,837	321,162	198,291
Total Operating Revenues	2,397,725	2,274,656	2,426,700	1,974,366	1,548,154	985,854	777,067
OPERATING EXPENSES							
Fort Wayne - City Lines	801,796	835,629	886,849	844,943	711,495	669,126	563,883
Wabash - City Lines	20,434	18,940	20,151	15,151	8,949	—	—
Peru - City Lines	24,366	21,773	21,172	16,906	13,237	13,163	10,853
Logansport - City Lines	91,785	80,345	82,623	76,210	54,817	23,528	—
Lafayette - City Lines	—	—	—	—	—	--	—
Interurban Lines	1,232,223	1,155,674	1,155,719	901,479	761,888	538,052	343,747
Total Operating Expenses	2,170,604	2,112,361	2,166,514	1,854,689	1,550,386	1,243,869	918,483
NET OPERATING INCOME							
Fort Wayne - City Lines	335,190	275,451	323,718	253,652	185,766	(33,495)	7,753
Wabash - City Lines	(5,384)	(3,717)	(5,859)	(5,841)	(3,837)	—	—
Peru - City Lines	(1,808)	4,318	4,242	2,255	245	(2,689)	(3,713)
Logansport - City Lines	(1,411)	3,522	1,858	(7,669)	(4,355)	(4,941)	—
Lafayette - City Lines	—	—	—	—	—	—	—
Interurban Lines	(99,466)	(117,279)	(63,773)	(122,720)	(180,051)	(216,890)	(145,456)
Total Net Operating Income	227,121	162,295	260,186	119,677	(2,232)	(258,015)	(141.416)

( ) Loss

INDIANA SERVICE CORPORATION

OPERATING REVENUES, OPERATING EXPENSES AND OPERATING INCOME
STREET AND INTERURBAN RAILWAY LINES
YEARS 1934 TO 1940, INCL.

	1934	1935	1936	1937	1938	1939	1940
OPERATING REVENUES							
Fort Wayne - City Lines	681,021	708,510	806,613	822,281	711,226	735,125	773,379
Wabash — City Lines	—	—	—	—	—	—	—
Peru — City Lines	7,448	—	—	—	—	—	—
Logansport - City Lines	—	—	—	—	—	—	—
Lafayette — City Lines	—	—	—	—	—	—	—
Interurban Lines	175,349	67,867	81,409	43,218	28,239	34,192	41,616
Total Operating Revenues	863,818	776,377	888,022	865,499	739,465	769,317	814,995
OPERATING EXPENSES							
Fort Wayne - City Lines	594,350	627,876	706,742	736,471	712,077	713,284	776,565
Wabash — City Lines	—	—	—	—	—	—	—
Peru — City Lines	10,028	—	—	—	—	—	—
Logansport - City Lines	—	—	—	—	—	—	—
Lafayette — City Lines	—	—	—	—	—	—	—
Interurban Lines	281,069	102,462	113,812	32,104	14,791	15,075	16,342
Total Operating Expenses	885,447	730,338	820,554	768,575	726,868	728,359	792,907
NET OPERATING INCOME							
Fort Wayne - City Lines	86,671	80,634	99,871	85,810	(851)	21,841	(3,186)
Wabash — City Lines	—	—	—	—	—	—	—
Peru — City Lines	(2,580)	—	—	—	—	—	—
Logansport - City Lines	—	—	—	—	—	—	. —
Lafayette — City Lines	—	—	—	—	—	—	—
Interurban Lines	(150,720)	(34,595)	(32,403)	11,114	13,448	19,117	25,274
Total Net Operating Income	(21,629)	46,039	67,468	96,924	12,597	40,958	22,088

( ) Loss

INDIANA SERVICE CORPORATION

OPERATING REVENUES, OPERATING EXPENSES AND OPERATING INCOME
STREET AND INTERURBAN RAILWAY LINES
YEARS 1941 TO 1947 INCL.

	1941	1942	1943	1944	1945	1946	1947
OPERATING REVENUES							
Fort Wayne - City Lines	855,589	1,152,992	1,510,242	1,601,965	1,546,277	1,443,571	1,595,799
Wabash - City Lines	—	—	—	—	—	—	—
Peru - City Lines	—	—	—	—	—	—	—
Logansport - City Lines	—	—	—	—	—	—	—
Lafayette - City Lines	—	—	—	—	—	—	—
Interurban Lines	41,036	68,339	42,140	44,594	22,330	18,427	22,964
Total Operating Revenues	890,625	1,221,331	1,552,382	1,646,559	1,568,607	1,461,998	1,618,763
OPERATING ESPENSES							
Fort Wayne - City Lines	746,001	917,308	1,246,468	1,322,561	1,359,603	1,233,732	1,427,542
Wabash - City Lines	—	—	—	—	—	—	—
Peru - City Lines	—	—	—	—	—	—	—
Logansport - City Lines	—	—	—	—	—	—	—
Lafayette - City Lines	—	—	—	—	—	—	—
Interurban Lines	19,737	49,324	46,288	43,113	14,364	9,694	12,048
Total Operating Expenses	765,738	966,632	1,292,756	1,365,674	1,373,967	1,243,426	1,439,590
NET OPERATING INCOME							
Fort Wayne - City Lines	109,588	235,684	263,774	279,404	186,674	209,839	168.256
Wabash - City Lines	—	—	—	—	—	—	—
Peru - City Lines	—	—	—	—	—	—	—
Logansport - City Lines	—	—	—	—	—	—	--
Lafayette - City Lines	—	—	—	—	—	—	—
Interurban Lines	21,299	19,015	(4,148)	1,481	7,966	8,733	10,915
Total Net Operating Income	130,887	254,699	259,626	280,885	194,640	218,572	179,171

( ) Loss

INDIANA SERVICE CORPORATION

CAR MILES AND PASSENGERS CARRIED
STREET AND INTERURBAN RAILWAY LINES
YEARS 1914 TO 1919, INCL.

	1914	1915	1916	1917	1918	1919
CAR MILES						
Fort Wayne - City Lines	2,098,453	2,034,648	2,257,108	2,447,344	2,201,377	Missing
Wabash - City Lines	116,175	106,663	91,825	91,559	89,752	Missing
Peru - City Lines	92,095	99,560	102,875	92,012	91,246	Missing
Logansport - City Lines	408,775	418,249	410,845	418,082	340,507	Missing
Lafayette - City Lines	751,450	822,404	800,794	795,646	725,409	Missing
Interurban Lines	1,323,876	1,260,267	1,246,819	1,241,541	1,086,956	Missing
Total Car Miles	4,790,824	4,741,791	4,910,266	5,086,184	4,535,247	Missing
PASSENGERS CARRIED						
Fort Wayne - City Lines	14,139,245	10,664,512	12,814,018	15,669,859	14,585,818	Missing
Wabash - City Lines	320,088	307,250	338,747	328,194	327,248	Missing
Peru - City Lines	375,376	239,769	210,823	207,678	296,325	Missing
Logansport - City Lines	1,773,424	1,585,095	1,193,575	1,421,840	1,467,240	Missing
Lafayette - City Lines	3,413,797	3,379,674	3,466,311	3,444,156	3,751,133	Missing
Interurban Lines	1,855,390	1,670,327	1,705,836	1,712,730	1,444,232	Missing
Total Passengers Carried	21,877,320	17,856,627	19,729,320	22,784,467	21,871,996	Missing

I. S. C. #68, later 168, at the Huntington shops. Freight cars like these were also built by I. S. C.'s mechanical staff.

INDIANA SERVICE CORPORATION

CAR MILES AND PASSENGERS CARRIED
STREET AND INTERURBAN RAILWAY LINES
YEARS 1920 TO 1926, INCL.

	1920	1921	1922	1923	1924	1925	1926
CAR MILES							
Fort Wayne - City Lines	2,388,187	2,676,006	2,901,021	3,163,338	3,353,204	3,425,372	3,458,601
Wabash - City Lines	93,349	95,583	96,144	93,636	92,567	95,290	95,513
Peru - City Lines	95,019	92,015	91,218	92,140	141,092	152,765	153,608
Logansport - City Lines	419,881	425,087	415,865	419,538	419,131	414,713	395,901
Lafayette - City Lines	244,679	—	—	—	—	—	—
Interurban Lines	1,564,879	1,431,497	1,496,758	1,670,556	1,888,605	2,377,930	2,662,929
Total Car Miles	4,805,994	4,720,188	5,001,006	5,439,208	5,894,599	6,466,070	6,766,552
PASSENGERS CARRIED							
Fort Wayne - City Lines	15,745,455	13,967,871	15,676,745	20,253,761	21,119,848	21,531,992	21,697,971
Wabash - City Lines	476,987	395,303	387,806	394,725	377,409	316,693	286,627
Peru - City Lines	436,305	337,311	310.864	319,635	490,545	459,885	450,540
Logansport - City Lines	2,727,402	2,499,128	2,371,669	2,445,831	2,241,070	2,088,084	1,982,607
Lafayette - City Lines	—	—	—	—	—	—	—
Interurban Lines	1,481,739	1,204,148	1,140,888	1,161,734	1,098,356	1,251,501	1,250,100
Total Passengers Carried	20,867,888	18,403,761	19,887,972	24,575,686	25,327,228	25,648,155	25,667,845

Production line methods were used in the construction of reinforced concrete poles at the McKinley yards. These poles were widely used in Fort Wayne.

INDIANA SERVICE CORPORATION

CAR MILES AND PASSENGERS CARRIED
STREET AND INTERURBAN RAILWAY LINES
YEARS 1927 TO 1933, INCL.

	1927	1928	1929	1930	1931	1932	1933
CAR MILES							
Fort Wayne - City Lines	3,388,081	3,541,957	3,736,826	3,735,913	3,596,426	3,368,123	3,171,489
Wabash - City Lines	104,249	115,977	113,651	78,744	51,467	—	—
Peru - City Lines	153,666	153,589	152,355	137,614	126,931	128,391	125,856
Logansport - City Lines	379,668	379,845	400,867	355,198	334,722	129,717	—
Lafayette - City Lines	—	—	—	—	—	—	—
Interurban Lines	2,929,889	2,795,695	2,964,343	2,822,317	2,531,580	1,495,094	1,029,403
Total Car Miles	6,955,553	6,987,063	7,368,042	7,129,786	6,641,126	5,121,325	4,326,748
PASSENGERS CARRIED							
Fort Wayne - City Lines	20,724,021	20,454,484	22,408,115	22,107,838	17,758,484	12,789,691	12,730,415
Wabash - City Lines	273,984	281,619	261,901	173,120	103,213	—	—
Peru - City Lines	447,730	518,370	504,382	379,810	276,705	218,295	151,878
Logansport - City Lines	1,764,825	1,646,040	1,636,615	1,469,582	1,116,647	412,456	—
Lafayette - City Lines	—	—	—	—	—	—	—
Interurban Lines	1,187,258	1,000,431	1,039,280	808,778	723,455	296,797	228,946
Total Passengers Carried	24,397,818	23,900,944	25,850,393	24,939,128	19,978,504	13,717,239	13,111,239

The 554 on the Taylor Street run, in June 1947 shortly before the end of streetcars in that same June 1947.

INDIANA SERVICE CORPORATION

CAR MILES AND PASSENGERS CARRIED
STREET AND INTERURBAN RAILWAY LINES
YEARS 1934 TO 1940, INCL.

	1934	1935	1936	1937	1938	1939	1940
CAR MILES							
Fort Wayne - City Lines	3,104,825	3,274,454	3,353,886	3,353,785	3,118,061	3,015,446	2,951,024
Wabash - City Lines	—	—	—	—	—	—	—
Peru - City Lines	117,770	—	—	—	—	—	—
Logansport - City Lines	—	—	—	—	—	—	—
Lafayette - City Lines	—	—	—	—	—	—	—
Interurban Lines	576,196	231,059	419,521	105,718	48,747	42,887	62,694
Total Car Miles	3,798,791	3,505,513	3,773,407	3,459,503	3,166,808	3,058,333	3,013,718
PASSENGERS CARRIED							
Fort Wayne - City Lines	15,048,100	15,506,966	17,513,673	18,041,107	15,568,071	16,022,157	16,927,433
Wabash - City Lines	—	—	—	—	—	—	—
Peru - City Lines	157,837	—	—	—	—	—	—
Logansport - City Lines	—	—	—	—	—	—	—
Lafayette - City Lines	—	—	—	—	—	—	—
Interurban Lines	260,499	113,376	147,211	18,410	—	—	—
Total Passengers Carried	15,466,436	15,620,342	17,660,884	18,059,517	15,568,071	16,022,157	16,927,433

The number 794 was assigned by Indiana R.R. to 821, although I. R. R. never used the car.

INDIANA SERVICE CORPORATION

CAR MILES AND PASSENGERS CARRIED
STREET AND INTERURBAN RAILWAY LINES
YEARS 1941 TO 1947, INCL.

	1941	1942	1943	1944	1945	1946	1947
CAR MILES							
Fort Wayne - City Lines	2,784,204	2,920,784	2,737,938	2,858,459	2,912,446	2,948,926	2,992,133
Wabash - City Lines	—	—	—	—	—	—	—
Peru - City Lines	—	—	—	—	—	—	—
Logansport - City Lines	—	—	—	—	—	—	—
Lafayette - City Lines	—	—	—	—	—	—	—
Interurban Lines	56,580	95,771	39,528	29,417	—	—	—
Total Car Miles	2,840,784	3,016,555	2,777,466	2,887,876	2,912,446	2,948,926	2,992,133
PASSENGERS CARRIED							
Fort Wayne - City Lines	18,377,795	25,322,670	34,130,150	36,249,538	34,823,578	32,289,034	31,738,103
Wabash - City Lines	—	—	—	—	—	—	—
Peru - City Lines	—	—	—	—	—	—	—
Logansport - City Lines	—	—	—	—	—	—	—
Lafayette - City Lines	—	—	—	--	—	—	—
Interurban Lines	—	—	—	—	—	—	—
Total Passengers Carried	18,377,795	25,322,670	34,130,150	36,249,538	34,823,578	32,289,034	31,738,103

I. S. C. #818 became Indiana R.R. #792. The center cab car was built from F. W. & N. W. passenger car #5. The location is the Fort Wayne freight terminal in August 1937.

PURDUE UNIVERSITY TEST CAR

Purdue University owned an interurban car used for testing purposes by the Electrical Engineering School. The car body was built by the J. G. Brill Company, in early 1903, and mounted on a special flat car. As such, and with the application of several vestibule ends of varying design it was run, as fast as possible (probably not above 60 m.p.h.) over several electric lines of the Union Traction Co. of Ind. This was a special series of tests run in conjunction with the Louisiana Purchase Exposition at St. Louis.

Following the close of the Exposition the car, as suplus, found a home at Purdue. It was rebuilt and mounted on high-speed Brill 27-E3 trucks. The work was probably done at the Wabash Valley's, Lafayette car barn. It emerged as the Purdue University Test Car, painted a golden yellow with black lettering and trim — including the university's seal.

Most of the tests were conducted on the local Battleground line but trips were occasionally made to Indianapolis and Fort Wayne. The latter runs over the Wabash Valley Lines. Outside of the electrified campus trackage the Wabash Valley route was the Purdue car's "home" territory.

Several other universities also owned similar cars which were later junked. Purdue's car, however, had the good fortune to be stored, after it's useful days were ended and it's last run completed in May, 1940, in the Purdue Locomotive Museum building.

After gathering dust for ten years, a drive was spear headed by George Bradley and the Purdue Railroad Club, with the able assistance of Dean A. A. Potter, to either re-open or transfer the collection to a new location. In October, 1951, the entire collection, including the test car and three very old locomotives, was shipped to the National Museum of Transport at St. Louis. Purdue's car is now a major display and is probably the oldest interurban car in existance.

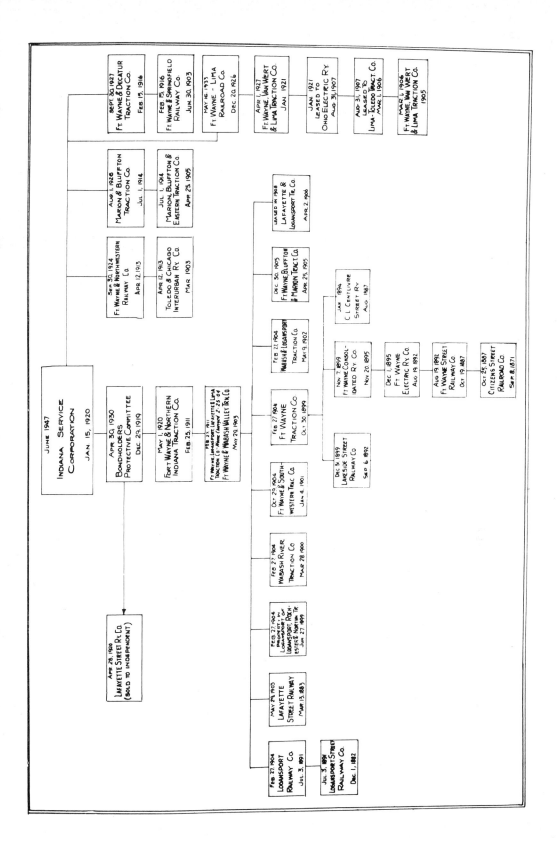

June 1947
INDIANA SERVICE CORPORATION
JAN. 15, 1920

BONDHOLDERS PROTECTIVE COMMITTEE
DEC. 23, 1919

APR. 30, 1930
LAFAYETTE STREET RY. CO.
(SOLD TO INDEPENDENT)
APR. 28, 1920

MAY 1, 1920
FORT WAYNE & NORTHERN INDIANA TRACTION CO.
FEB. 25, 1911

FEB. 27, 1911
FT. WAYNE, LOGANSPORT, LAFAYETTE & LIMA TRACTION CO. – NOW CONTROL 2, 26 OF
FT. WAYNE & WABASH VALLEY TRAC. CO.
MAY 29, 1905

SEPT. 30, 1924
FT. WAYNE & NORTHWESTERN RAILWAY CO.
APR. 12, 1913

APR. 12, 1913
TOLEDO & CHICAGO INTERURBAN RY. CO.
MAR. 1903

AUG. 1, 1926
MARION & BLUFFTON TRACTION CO.
JUL. 1, 1914

JUL. 1, 1914
MARION, BLUFFTON & EASTERN TRACTION CO.
APR. 25, 1905

SEPT. 30, 1927
FT. WAYNE & DECATUR TRACTION CO.
FEB. 15, 1916

FEB. 15, 1916
FT. WAYNE & SPRINGFIELD RAILWAY CO.
JUN. 30, 1903

MAY 16, 1933
FT. WAYNE – LIMA RAILROAD CO.
DEC. 20, 1926

APR. 1, 1927
FT. WAYNE, VAN WERT & LIMA TRACTION CO.
JAN. 1921

JAN. 1921
LEASED TO OHIO ELECTRIC RY.
AUG. 31, 1907

AUG. 31, 1907
LEASED TO LIMA - TOLEDO TRACT. CO.
MAR. 1, 1906

MAR. 1, 1906
FT. WAYNE, VAN WERT & LIMA TRACTION CO.
1905

LEASED IN 1908
LAFAYETTE & LOGANSPORT TR. CO.
APR. 2, 1906

DEC. 30, 1905
FT. WAYNE, BLUFFTON & MARION TRACT. CO.
APR. 25, 1905

FEB. 27, 1904
WABASH & LOGANSPORT TRACTION CO.
MAY 9, 1902

FEB. 27, 1904
FT. WAYNE TRACTION CO.
OCT. 30, 1899

JAN. 1894
C L CENTLIVRE STREET RY
AUG. 1887

NOV. 7, 1899
FT. WAYNE CONSOLIDATED RY. CO.
NOV. 20, 1895

DEC. 1, 1895
FT. WAYNE ELECTRIC RY. CO.
AUG. 19, 1892

AUG. 19, 1892
FT. WAYNE STREET RAILWAY CO.
OCT. 19, 1887

OCT. 25, 1867
CITIZENS STREET RAILROAD CO.
SEP. 8, 1871

DEC. 31, 1899
LAKESIDE STREET RAILWAY CO.
SEP. 6, 1892

OCT. 29, 1904
FT. WAYNE & SOUTHWESTERN TRAC. CO.
JAN. 4, 1901

FEB. 27, 1904
WABASH RIVER TRACTION CO.
MAR. 28, 1900

FEB. 27, 1904
PROPERTY OF LOGANSPORT, ROCHESTER & NORTHERN TR.
JUN. 27, 1899

MAY 29, 1903
LAFAYETTE STREET RAILWAY
MAR. 13, 1883

FEB. 27, 1904
LOGANSPORT RAILWAY CO.
JUL. 3, 1891

JUL. 3, 1891
LOGANSPORT STREET RAILWAY CO.
DEC. 1, 1882

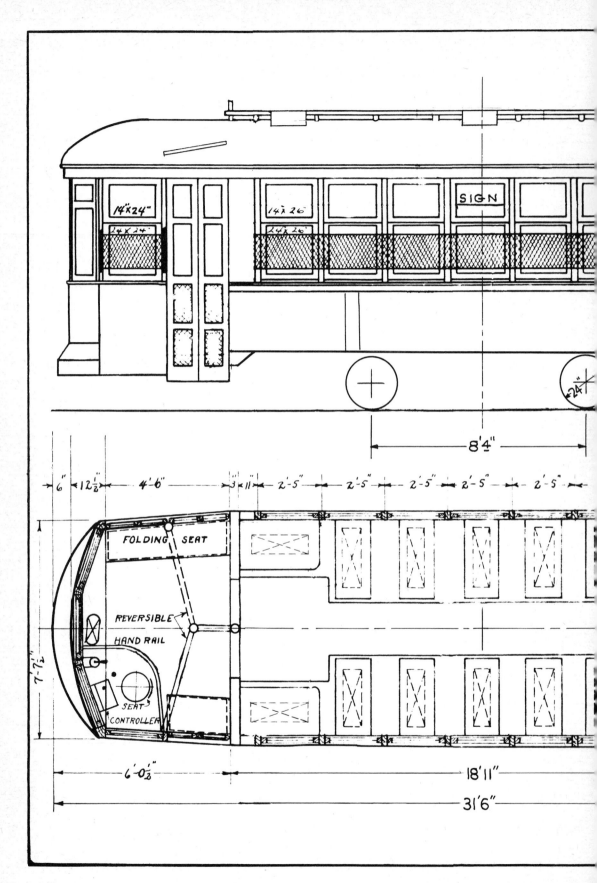

14"x24"

14"X 24"

14"x 26"

14"x 26"

SIGN

24"

8'4"

6" 12½" 4'-6" 3"11" 2'-5" 2'-5" 2'-5" 2'-5" 2'-5"

FOLDING SEAT

REVERSIBLE

HAND RAIL

SEAT

CONTROLLER

7'-7½"

6'-0½"

18'11"

31'6"

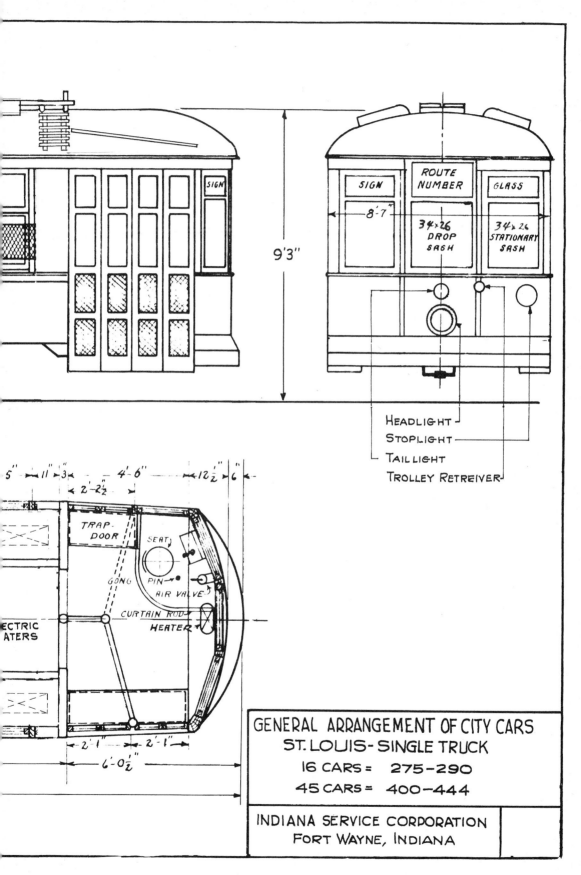

9'3"

SIGN

ROUTE NUMBER
SIGN
GLASS

8'-7"

34×26 DROP SASH
34×26 STATIONARY SASH

HEADLIGHT
STOPLIGHT
TAIL LIGHT
TROLLEY RETREIVER

5" 11" 3" 4'-6" 12½" 6"
2'-2½"

TRAP DOOR
SEAT
GONG
PIN
AIR VALVE
CURTAIN ROD
HEATER

ELECTRIC HEATERS

2'-1" 2'-1"
6'-0½"

GENERAL ARRANGEMENT OF CITY CARS
ST. LOUIS - SINGLE TRUCK
16 CARS = 275-290
45 CARS = 400-444

INDIANA SERVICE CORPORATION
FORT WAYNE, INDIANA

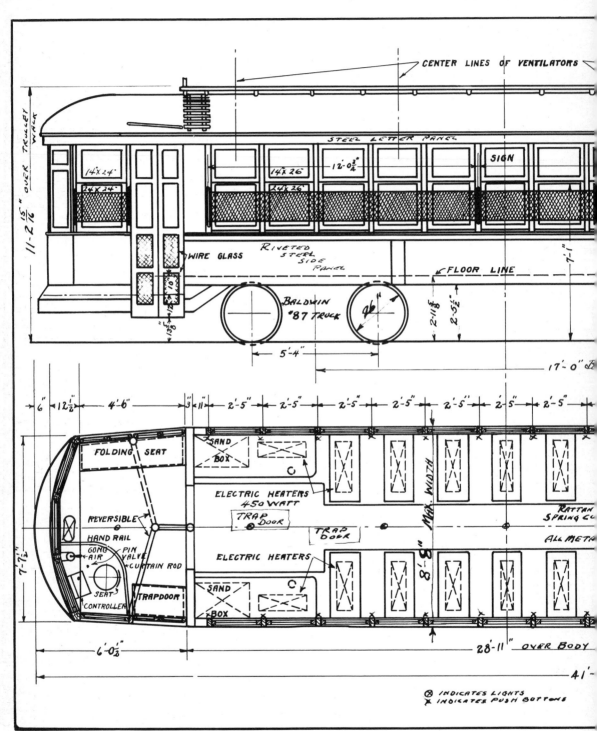

CENTER LINES OF VENTILATORS

STEEL LETTER PANEL

SIGN

14"x24"

14"x26"   12'-0¾"

24"x24"   24"x26"

WIRE GLASS

RIVETED STEEL SIDE PANEL

FLOOR LINE

7'-1"

BALDWIN "87 TRUCK

2-11⅝"

2'-5½"

5'-4"

17'-0"

11'-2 15/16" OVER TROLLEY WALK

6" 12½"   4'-6"   3' 11"   2'-5"   2'-5"   2'-5"   2'-5"   2'-5"   2'-5"   2'-5"

FOLDING   SEAT

SAND BOX

ELECTRIC HEATERS 450 WATT

TRAP DOOR

MAX. WIDTH

RATTAN SPRING C⁻

REVERSIBLE

TRAP DOOR

ALL METAL

HAND RAIL

GONG   PIN
AIR   VALVE
       CURTAIN ROD

ELECTRIC HEATERS

SEAT
CONTROLLER   TRAPDOOR

SAND BOX

8'-3"

7'-7½"

6'-0½"

28'-11" OVER BODY

41'-

⊗ INDICATES LIGHTS
✗ INDICATES PUSH BOTTONS

TAKEN FROM ST. LOUIS CAR CO. B/P DRAWING NO. 443-2038

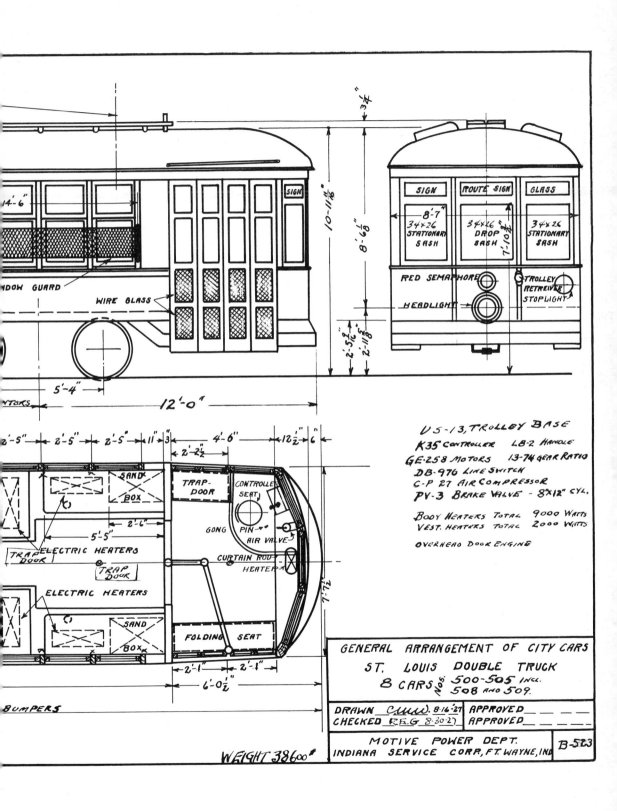

14'-6"

SIGN

10-11⅛"

8'-6⅝"

3¾"

WINDOW GUARD

WIRE GLASS

5'-4"

12'-0"

2'-5²⁄₁₆"
2'-11⅝"

7'-10⅞"

SIGN	ROUTE SIGN	GLASS
8'-7 34×26 STATIONARY SASH	34×26 DROP SASH	34×26 STATIONARY SASH

RED SEMAPHORE

HEADLIGHT

TROLLEY RETRIEVER STOPLIGHT

2'-5" · 2'-5" · 2'-5" · 11" · 3" · 4'-6" · 12½" · 6"

2'-2½"

SAND BOX

TRAP DOOR

CONTROLLER SEAT

2'-6"

5'-5"

TRAP DOOR

ELECTRIC HEATERS

GONG

PIN AIR VALVE

CURTAIN ROD HEATER

TRAP DOOR

ELECTRIC HEATERS

SAND BOX

FOLDING SEAT

7'-7½"

2'-1" · 2'-1"

6'-0½"

BUMPERS

WEIGHT 38600#

US-13, TROLLEY BASE
K-35 CONTROLLER   LB-2 HANDLE
GE-258 MOTORS   13-74 GEAR RATIO
DB-976 LINE SWITCH
C-P 27 AIR COMPRESSOR
PV-3 BRAKE VALVE - 8"×12" CYL.

BODY HEATERS TOTAL 9000 WATTS
VEST. HEATERS TOTAL 2000 WATTS

OVERHEAD DOOR ENGINE

GENERAL ARRANGEMENT OF CITY CARS
ST. LOUIS DOUBLE TRUCK
8 CARS Nos. 500-505 INCL.
508 AND 509.

DRAWN CHN 8-16-27	APPROVED _ _ _ _
CHECKED R.E.G 8-30-27	APPROVED _ _ _ _

MOTIVE POWER DEPT.
INDIANA SERVICE CORP., FT. WAYNE, IND

B-523

165

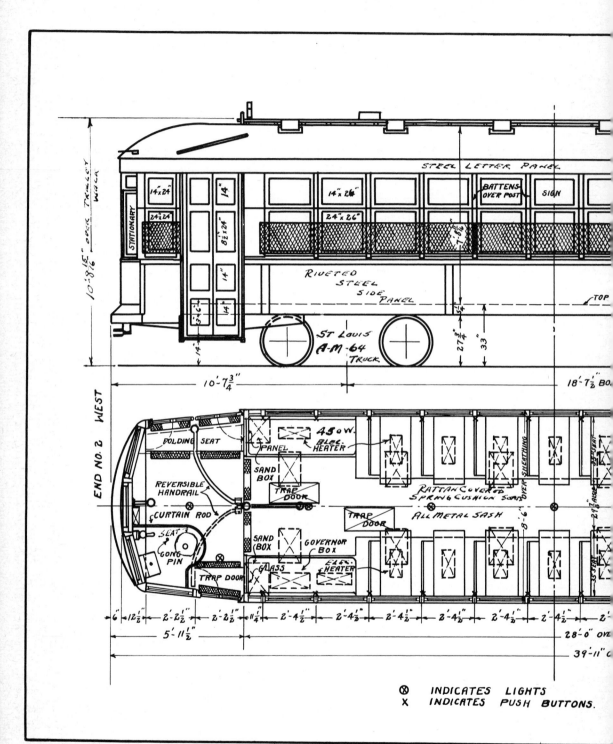

STEEL LETTER PANEL

14"x24"
24"x24"
14"
8½x24"
14"
14"
3'-6"
14"x26"
24"x26"
14"
BATTENS OVER POST
SIGN
STATIONARY

RIVETED STEEL SIDE PANEL

TOP

ST LOUIS
A-M-64
TRUCK

27¾"
33"

10'-8 15/16" OVER TROLLEY WORK

10'-7¾"
18'-7½" BO

END NO. 2 WEST

FOLDING SEAT
REVERSIBLE HANDRAIL
CURTAIN ROD
SEAT
GONG PIN
TRAP DOOR

PANEL
SAND BOX
TRAP DOOR
SAND BOX
GLASS

450 W. ELEC. HEATER
GOVERNOR BOX
TRAP DOOR
ELEC. HEATER

RATTAN COVERED SPRING CUSHION SEAT
ALL METAL SASH
OVER SHEATHING

6" 12½" 2'-2½" 2'-2½" 11¼" 2'-4½" 2'-4½" 2'-4½" 2'-4½" 2'-4½" 2'-4½" 2'-
5'-11½"
28'-0" OVE
39'-11" O

⊗ INDICATES LIGHTS
X INDICATES PUSH BUTTONS.

COPIED FROM ST. LOUIS CAR CO. B/P 443-2078

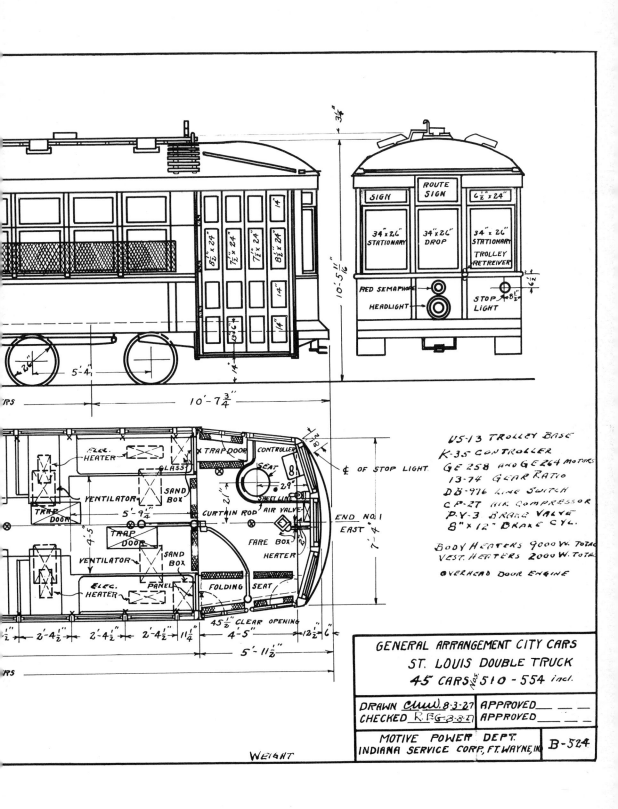

SIGN · **ROUTE SIGN** · $6\frac{1}{2}$" × 24"

34" × 26" STATIONARY · 34" × 26" DROP · 34" × 26" STATIONARY TROLLEY RETRIEVER

RED SEMAPHORE · HEADLIGHT · STOP LIGHT

$8\frac{1}{2}$" × 24" · $7\frac{1}{2}$" × 24" · $7\frac{1}{2}$" × 24" · $8\frac{1}{2}$" × 24" · 14"

14" · $13\frac{1}{4}$" · 14" · 14"

10'-5$\frac{11}{16}$"

3$\frac{3}{4}$"

26" · 5'-4" · 10'-7$\frac{3}{4}$"

ELEC. HEATER · TRAP DOOR · CONTROLLER
GLASS · SEAT · ¢ OF STOP LIGHT
VENTILATOR · SAND BOX · SHEET LINE · 29" · 21" · 2"
TRAP DOOR · CURTAIN ROD · AIR VALVE · END NO I EAST
5'-9$\frac{1}{4}$" · FARE BOX · HEATER
4'-5 · TRAP DOOR · 7'-4"
VENTILATOR · SAND BOX
ELEC. HEATER · PANEL · FOLDING SEAT
45$\frac{1}{2}$" CLEAR OPENING
$\frac{1}{2}$" · 2'-4$\frac{1}{2}$" · 2'-4$\frac{1}{2}$" · 2'-4$\frac{1}{2}$" · 11$\frac{1}{4}$" · 4'-5" · 12$\frac{1}{2}$" · 6"
5'-11$\frac{1}{2}$"

US-13 TROLLEY BASE
K-35 CONTROLLER
GE 258 AND GE 264 MOTORS
13-74 GEAR RATIO
DB-976 LINE SWITCH
CP-27 AIR COMPRESSOR
P-Y-3 BRAKE VALVE
8" × 12" BRAKE CYL.

BODY HEATERS 9000 W. TOTAL
VEST. HEATERS 2000 W. TOTAL

OVERHEAD DOOR ENGINE

WEIGHT

GENERAL ARRANGEMENT CITY CARS		
ST. LOUIS DOUBLE TRUCK		
45 CARS Nos. 510 - 554 incl.		
DRAWN CMW 8-3-27	APPROVED ___ __ _	
CHECKED RFG-3-8-27	APPROVED ___ __ _	
MOTIVE POWER DEPT. INDIANA SERVICE CORP. FT. WAYNE, IND		B-524

167

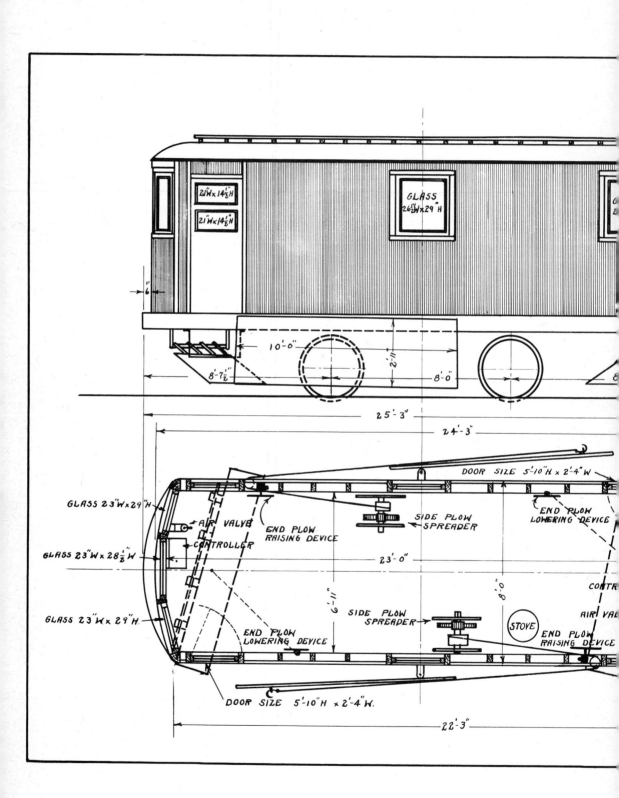

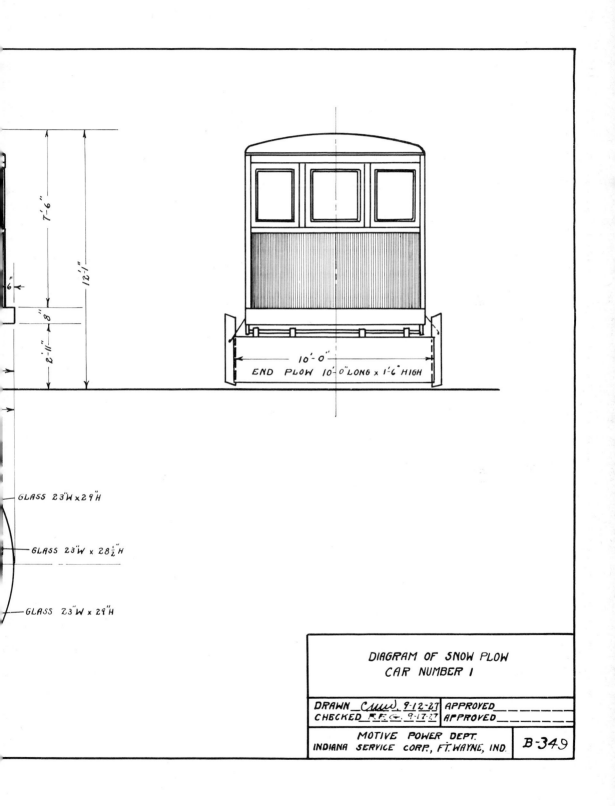

7'-6"

12'-1"

6"

8"

2'-11"

GLASS 23"W x 29"H

GLASS 23"W x 28½"H

GLASS 23"W x 29"H

10'-0"

END PLOW 10'-0" LONG x 1'-6" HIGH

DIAGRAM OF SNOW PLOW
CAR NUMBER 1

DRAWN _C_ _9-12-27_   APPROVED _____

CHECKED _R.F.G._ _9-17-27_   APPROVED _____

MOTIVE POWER DEPT.
INDIANA SERVICE CORP., FT. WAYNE, IND.

B-349

Notes

NOTES

CHAPTER ONE

1. Griswold, B. J., *History of Fort Wayne and Allen County*, Vol. 1, page 343.
2. F. W. & W. V. Tr. Co., - *Ordinance and Other Records*, pages 68-70.
3. Ibid, pages 70-72.
4. Fort Wayne "Sentinel" - January 7, 1872.
5. F. W. & W. V. Traction Co., *Ordinances and Others Records*, page 73.
6. Ibid, pages 73-74.
7. Fort Wayne "Sentinel" - Date unknown. The quote was taken as a direct quotation in an old letter written in 1892.
8. F. W. & W. V. Tr. Co., *Ordinances and Other Records*, page 85.
9. Ibid, pages 75-84.
10. Ibid, pages 86-94, - The complete record of the Court's decision and execution.
11. Ibid, pages 95-97, Incorporation of Fort Wayne Street Railroad showing the exact holdings of all interested parties.
12. Ibid, pages 127-140, Dealing with the streets in the City of Fort Wayne, the roads in Allen County and two bridges created a number of legal hurdles for the Centlivre Co.
13. Ibid 98-109, these extensions were dealt with seperately before the City Council to insure the passage of each.
14. —— *The Fort Wayne Code of 1931*, page XXI. A list of street name changes in Fort Wayne.
15. Griswold, B. J., *History of Fort Wayne and Allen County*, Vol. 1, pages 524-525.
16. F. W. & W. V. Tr. Co., *Ordinance and Other Records*, page 163-168.
17. Ibid, page 141-150.

CHAPTER TWO

1. Fort Wayne "Gazette", July 7, 1892.
2. F. W. & W. V. Tr. Co., *Ordinances and Other Records*, pages 122-124. The mortgage and bond issuance is clearly stated.
3. Griswold, B. J., *History of Fort Wayne and Allen County*, Vol. 1, pages 525-526.
4. F. W. & W. V. Tr. Co., *Ordinances and Other Records*, pages 160-162.
5. *Fort Wayne Up-to-Date 1874-1894. Twentieth Anniversary Issue of the Fort Wayne Daily News.*
6. Bates, Roy M., *Interurban Railways of Allen County*, pages 14-15.
7. F. W. & W. V. Tr. Co., *Ordinances and Other Records*, pages 170-173. The new company was more of a recapitalization and expansion of the old company than the introduction of an entirely different corporation.

CHAPTER THREE

1. Griswold, B. J., *History of Fort Wayne and Allen County*, pages 283,307.
2. F. W. & W. V. Tr. Co., *Ordinances and Other Records*, pages 174-180. Permission to use right-of-way along the side of the Leo Road and the crossing of the Feeder Canal on the County's bridge became quite involved.
3. Bates, R. M., *Robison Park 1896-1919*, pages 9-14. An excellent record of this important park, based on personal memories backed with facts.
4. F. W. & W. V. Tr. Co., *Ordinances and Other Records*, pages 181-220. This very lengthy decision on and disposition of the Consolidated Company produced some interesting and almost humorous side lights, in retrospect, of the scramble to take over the Company assests and who actually had some of these assests.
5. Ibid, pages 220-222. The Knickerbocker Company must have loaned the initial money, on a personal basis, to McDonald who in turn put the company proceeds in his own holdings. The car-line was practically worthless from a dollar view point.

CHAPTER FOUR

1. F. W. & W. V. Tr. Co., *Ordinances and Other Records*, pages 304-309. The city routing of the interurban, entirely seperate of the street railway operation, has been virtually forgotten by everybody, as it was only used for about three years.
2. Ibid. Pages 268-277.
3. Hilton, G. W. and Due, J. F., *The Electric Interurban Railways in America*, pages 26, 32.
4. F. W. & W. V. Tr. Co., *Ordinances and Other Records*, pages 332-337.
5. Ibid. Pages 310-311, 257-258. The corporate background and record of sales of the successive chain of power companies.
6. Ibid. Pages 360-369, 403-405.
7. Hilton, G. W. and Due, J. F., *The Electric Interurban Railways in America*, pages 96-97.
8. Ibid. Pages 58-59, 162.
9. —— *Inventory and Appraisal May 1, 1920 - Railway Utility*, pages 169-171.
10. Griswold, B. J., *History of Fort Wayne and Allen County*, Vol. 1, page 54.
11. —— *Fort Wayne & Wabash Valley Traction and Terminal Co., Consolidation Proposal - 1910.*
12. Hilton, G. W. and Due, J. F., *The Electric Interurban Railways in America*, pages 88-89.

CHAPTER FIVE

1. Hilton, G. W. and Due, J. F., *The Electric Interurban Railways in America*, page 282.
2. —— F. W. & N. I. Tr. Co., *Inventory and Appraisal of Railway Property as of January 1, 1918*, page 2-9.
3. Chambers, D. W., *Lafayette Street Railway*, page 16-17.
4. Fuestel, R. M., F. W. & N. I. Tr. Co., *Report of the Operating and Investment Data 1918*.

CHAPTER SIX

1. Hilton, G. W. and Due, J. F., *The Electric Interurban Railways in America*, pages 264-265, 282.
2. —— *Indiana Railroad System*, C. E. R. A. Bulletin 91, page 17.
3. Hilton, G. W. and Due, J. F., *The Electric Interurban Railways in America*, page 280.
4. F. W. & W. V. Tr. Co., *Ordinances and Other Records*, pages 497-502. Details of the Pearl Street freight station.
5. Bates, R. M., *Interurban Railways of Allen County*, page 25-27.
6. Hilton, G. W. and Due, J. F., *The Electric Interurban Railways in America*, pages 283-284.

CHAPTER SEVEN

1. F. W. & N. I. Tr. Co., *Operating Statistics 1904-1918*, page 21-22.
2. —— *The Fort Wayne Code of 1913*, page XXIX.
3. Much of this information was taken from two company track maps, dated 1922 and 1929, and from dated negatives made with the company's Kodak "autographic" camera.

CHAPTER EIGHT

1. —— *The Indiana Service Corporation*. A brochure issued by the I. S. C. at the time of the completion of the Spy Run facilities.
2. Ibid. pages not numbered.
3. —— *Inventory and Appraisal May 1, 1920 - Railway Utility*, page 169. The Glasgow Avenue property is not listed in the 1926 inventory.

CHAPTER NINE

1. Information used in Chapter 9 was gathered from statistics, files and company records of Fort Wayne Transit, Inc. and Indiana & Michigan Electric Co. None of this, being fairly recent or current, has been published except as news stories.

CHAPTER TEN

1. F. W. & N. I. Tr. Co., *Inventory and Appraisal of Railway Property as of January 1, 1918*, page 25-27.
2. Ibid. page 28, 34.
3. Ibid. page 13-17.
4. I. S. C., *Operating and Investment Data - City Lines 1919*, page 3.

CHAPTER ELEVEN

1. F. W. & W. V. Tr. Co., *Ordinances and Other Records*, page 195.
2. F. W. & N. I. Tr. Co., *Operating Statistics 1904-1918*, page 25A.
3. —— *Inventory and Appraisal May 1, 1920 - Railway Utility*, page 182-193.
4. Ibid. page 182-193.
5. Post 1940 information came from records of Fort Wayne Transit, Inc.
6. Interurban records for this section were taken from material in the possession of Indiana & Michigan Electric Co. and one copy of the I. S. C. 1920 Inventory which the mechanical department kept up-to-date with penciled notes.
7. F. W. & N. I. Tr. Co., *Inventory and Appraisal of Railway Property as of January 1, 1918*. page 27-28.
8. Chambers, D. W., *Lafayette Street Railway*, page 18.
9. —— *Inventory and Appraisal May 1, 1920 - Railway Utility*. The equipment roster uses the 1920 inventory, the most complete available, as a base point. Data on equipment built, purchased or acquired after 1920 was taken from the records of Fort Wayne Transit, Inc. and Indiana & Michigan Electric Co.

CHAPTER TWELVE

1. F. W. & N. I. Tr. Co., *Operating Statistics 1904-1918*, page 27. For some, now unknown, reason expenses and net income were given in a consolidated form from 1914-1917. The 1919 car miles records are lost. All figures from 1920-1947 were prepared by Indiana & Michigan Electric Co.

Bibliography

SECTION I BOOKS AND PAMPHLETS

R. M. Bates, *Interurban Railways of Allen County Indiana,* (Fort Wayne: Public Library 1958).

R. M. Bates, *Robison Park 1896-1919,* (2nd Edition), (Fort Wayne: Old Fort News Vol. XIX, No. 2, Allen County-Fort Wayne Historical Society, 1956).

D. W. Chambers, *Lafayette Street Railway,* (Chicago: Bulletin #32 of the Electric Railway Historical Society, 1958).

B. J. Griswold, *History of Fort Wayne and Allen County,* (Chicago: Robert O. Law Co., 1917) Volume 1, only.

G. W. Hilton and J. F. Due, *The Electric Interurban Railways in America,* (Stanford, Stanford University Press, 1960).

F. Rowsome, Jr., *Trolley Car Treasury,* (New York: McGraw-Hill, 1956).

—— *The Fort Wayne Code of 1931,* (Fort Wayne: City of Fort Wayne, 1931).

—— *Fort Wayne Up-to-Date, 1874-1894,* (Fort Wayne: Twentieth Aniversary of the Fort Wayne Daily News, 1894).

—— *Indiana Railroad System,* (Chicago: Bulletin 91 of the Central Electric Railfans Association, 1950).

—— *Indiana Service Corporation,* (Fort Wayne: a booklet printed by I. S. C., 1926).

SECTION II COMPANY AND PRIVATE PAPERS

Fort Wayne and Wabash Valley Traction and Terminal Company Consolidation Proposal, 1910.

Fort Wayne and Northern Indiana Traction Company - Operating Statistics, 1904-1918. (A detailed study of why the company was failing and about to go into recievership).

Fort Wayne and Northern Indiana Traction Company. Inventory and Appraisal of Railway Property as of January 1, 1918. (The complete record of the interurban and street railway line in detail).

R. M. Fuestel, *Fort Wayne and Northern Indiana Traction Company - Report of the Operating and Investment Data, 1918.* (A detailed report by the company president).

Indiana Service Corporation, *Operating and Investment Data - City Lines, 1919.*

Inventory and Appraisal May 1, 1920 - Railway Utility, Indiana Service Corporation, Fort Wayne, Indiana. (The complete inventory and valuation. The copy used by the author had been in the mechanical department and carefully annotated with additional dates and information until late in 1926).

Inventory 1926 - Railway Utility, Indiana Service Corporation, Fort Wayne, Indiana.

Fort Wayne & Wabash Valley Traction Company - Ordinances and Other Records 1906. Vol. 1 (A compilation of legal documents prepared by the General Counsel. This is a typed record, several copies made, of all deeds, court actions, City Council proceedings and County Commissioners records, from their several records, of all action pertaining to the company and it's predecessors from 1870-1906.

SECTION III NEWSPAPERS AND PERIODICALS

Transit Journal, and it's predecessor publications from the McGraw Publishing Company, covering a period from 1896 through 1940.

Fort Wayne Journal-Gazette. Contemporary accounts of actions and happenings from 1879 to the present.

Fort Wayne News-Sentinel. Contemporary accounts of actions and happenings from 1870 to the present.

Index

Abandonments - 43, 51, 53, 60, 61.
Accidents - 39, 41, 42, 43, 51.
A. C. electrification - 33, 39, 43, 44.
Allen County - 11.
Allen County-Fort Wayne Historical Society - 98.
American Car Co. - 109.
American Electric Power Co. - 93.
American Electric Railway Association - 125.
American Gas & Electric Co. - 93.
"Anthony Wayne" - 128.
Atlantic City Transportation Co. - 117, 121.
Auburn, Ind. - 39.
Aveline House - 9.

Baker St. *(South Barns)* - 13, 71, 81, 109, 135.
Baldwin trucks - 123.
Barney & Smith Co. - 109.
Barrett, J. M. - 11.
Bass, J. H. - 9, 11, 25, 26.
Bass Foundry - 18.
Battery Cars - 14.
Battleground Line - 47, 51, 109, 135.
Belt Line - 12, 19, 89.
Berne, Ind. - 43.
Block signals - 42.
Bloomingdale - 11.
Bloomingdale Line - 11, 17, 19.
Bluffton, Ind. - 31, 33, 41, 42, 60, 61, 81, 128.
Bluffton, Geneva & Celina Tr. Co. - 33, 39, 43, 145.
Boating - 25.
Bond, A. S. - 11.
Bond, S. B. - 9, 11.
Bondholders Protective Committee - 49, 51.
Boyd Park - 29, 38, 47, 81, 109, 113, 123, 135.
Brady, A. W. - 36.
Breckenridge, C. - 9.
Bridges - 11, 12, 14, 19, 23, 25, 31, 47, 58, 88, 99.
Brill, J. G., Co. - 45, 109, 110, 121, 160.
Broadway Line - 12, 31, 45, 67, 89.
Bryan, Ohio - 39.
Bueter Rd. - 67.
Buffalo, N. Y. - 121.
Bursley, G. E. - 9.
Buses, City, Motor - 83, 89, 95, 121.
Buses, City, Trolley - 83, 88, 95, 98, 121.
Buses, Intercity - 53, 60, 121, 147.

Calhoun St. Line - 9, 14, 45, 67, 71, 95.
"Canal Route" - 27.
Cars, new closed - 9, 11, 13, 17, 23, 45, 48, 63, 105, 109.
Cars, new open - 18, 23, 49, 107, 109.
Cars, new double truck - 48, 63, 109, 113.
Cars, new interurban - 31, 44, 51, 53, 58, 60, 123, 125, 128, 130.
Cars, new parlor-buffett - 31, 53, 123, 128.
Cars, office - 36, 123.
Cars, service - 130, 135.
Car Barns - 9, 13, 14, 17, 36, 37, 38.
Carbaugh, F. - 93.
Centlivre, C. L. - 11.

Centlivre Brewery - 11, 93.
Centlivre Park - 12, 18, 23.
Centlivre Short Line - 49, 83.
Centlivre St. Ry. - 12, 14, 17, 18, 105.
Central Electric Railroads Association - 56.
Central High School - 88.
Chestnut St. Barns - 9, 13, 44, 109.
Chestnut St. Powerhouse - 17, 39.
Chicago, South Shore & South Bend R.R. - 128.
Church of the Good Shephard - 13.
Cincinnati Car Co. - 31, 109, 110, 123.
Cincinnati St. Ry. Co. - 29.
Citizens' St R.R. Co. - 9, 11, 105.
City Filtration Plant - 93.
City Light - 39.
Clementina - 25.
Cleveland, Ohio - 25, 125.
Coldwater, Mich. - 53.
Columbia City, Ind. - 19, 39.
Columbia St. Line - 14.
Commerce Drive - 56.
Corkwell, B. T. - 42.
Cornwall St. Ry. - 117.
County Commissioners - 11, 12.
"County Seat Trains" - 128.
Courts - 11, 25, 26.
Curtis trucks - 109, 113, 123.

Dam *(Feeder Canal)* - 21.
D. C. electrification - 33, 44, 81, 95.
Decatur, Ind. - 33, 44.
Delta Lake - 14.
Detroit, Mich. - 25.
Dorner truck - 105.
Driving Park - 14.
Dudlo Mfg. Co. - 67.

East Barn *(Glasgow Ave.)* - 13, 14, 17, 81, 88, 105.
East Creighton Line - 83, 95.
East State Line - 67, 71, 83, 93, 95, 135.
East Washington Line - 9, 17, 71, 83, 93.
Eel River - 38.
Elder, B. - 61.
Electrification - 17, 33.
Episcopal Church - 13.
Erie R.R. - 36, 41.
Everett, C. E. - 19.

Fairgrounds - 9.
Feeder Canal - 14, 21, 25, 75.
Feeder Dam - 21.
Feustel, R. M. - 48, 49, 51.
Fire Department - 14.
Ford, H. - 36.
Fort Wayne, Ind. - 9, 13, 21, 26, 27, 39, 51, 53, 58, 63, 88, 93, 95, 109, 160.
Ft. Wayne, Bluffton & Marion Tr. Co. - 31.
Fort Wayne City Lines - 44, 47, 60, 63, 83, 149.
Ft. Wayne Consolidated Ry. Co. - 19, 23, 25, 26, 107.

Ft. Wayne & Decatur Tr. Co. - 44, 53, 71, 125, 143.
Ft. Wayne Electric Light & Power Co. - 29.
Ft. Wayne Electric Ry. Co. - 17-19, 25-26, 105.
Ft. Wayne Electric Works - 14, 18, 26.
Ft. Wayne Fair - 41.
Ft. Wayne-Lima R.R. - 51, 60, 67, 71, 125, 147.
Ft. Wayne, Logansport, Lafayette & Lima Tr. Co. - 28, 123.
Ft. Wayne & Northern Indiana Tr. Co. - 42, 44, 45, 48, 51, 110, 113, 125.
Ft. Wayne & Northwestern Ry. Co. - 43, 51, 125, 143.
Ft. Wayne & Southwestern Tr. Co. - 27-29, 31, 38, 45, 123.
Ft. Wayne & Springfield Ry. Co. - 28, 33, 39, 44, 143.
Ft. Wayne St. R.R. - 11-12, 14, 17, 105.
Ft. Wayne Traction Co. - 26, 28, 29, 45, 105, 109.
Ft. Wayne Transit, Inc. - 93, 95, 98, 121.
Ft. Wayne, Van Wert & Lima Tr. Co. - 28, 31, 51, 145.
Ft. Wayne & Wabash Valley Tr. Co. - 28-29, 31, 36, 39, 41-42, 56, 103, 109, 123, 160.
Ft. Wayne & Wabash Valley Traction and Terminal Co. - 39.
Ft. Wayne Water Power Co. - 75.
Ft. Wayne & Winnona Tr. Co. - 39.
Freight cars - 143, 147.
Freight terminal - 56, 58.

Garrett, Ind. - 33, 61, 110, 149.
Garrettson, G. H. - 26.
General Electric Co. - 26.
Geneva, Ind. - 33.
Germania Park - 25.
Glasgow Ave. - 13, 81.
Grand Rapids & Indiana R.R. - 33.
Grand Union crossing - 83.
"Great Epizootic" - 9, 89.
Guaranty and Indemnity Trust Co. - 17, 25.
Guardian Trust Co. - 25.

Hanna, S. T. - 9.
Hanna St. Line - 12, 19.
Harvester Loop - 67, 71.
Hicksville, Ohio - 19.
Hicksville Rd. (East State) - 14.
"Hoosierland" - 31, 128.
Hosey, W. J. - 39.
Huffman St. Line - 45, 67.
Huntington, Ind. - 21, 27, 29, 99.
Huntington car shop - 36, 81, 123, 125, 135.

Inca Mfg. Co. - 71.
Indiana - 31, 60, 98.
"Indiana Flyer" - 128.
Indiana & Michigan Electric Co. - 93.
Indianapolis, Ind. - 25, 29, 121, 123, 160.
Indiana Service Corporation - 51, 53, 56, 58, 60-61, 63, 75, 81, 93, 99, 101, 103, 110, 125, 128, 130, 149.
Indiana Railroad - 60, 61, 99, 101, 103, 125, 128, 130, 125, 149.
Indiana Railroad Commission - 42-43.
Indiana Union Traction (See Union Traction)
Insull, S. - 53, 60.

International Harvester Co. - 67.
Interurbans - 27, 33, 39, 53, 60, 61.

Jackson and Sharp Co. - 123.
Jefferson Line - 9, 19.
Jenny Electric Light Co. - 9, 14.
Jenny Electric Light & Power Co. - 14, 31, 71.
Jitney buses - 47.
Jones, J. L. - 29.
Jones, J. M., Co. - 17, 105, 107, 109.
Junior Chamber of Commerce (Jaycees) - 98.
Justus, L. C. - 33, 41, 43.

Kamm St. Station - 14, 31, 39, 75, 113.
Kendallville, Ind. - 33, 39, 125.
Kingsland, Ind. - 31.
Kingsland wreck - 41-42, 123.
Knickerbocker Trust Co. - 26.
Kossuth St. barn - 113, 135.

Lafayette, Ind. - 38, 39, 47, 60, 99, 103, 109, 110, 135.
Lafayette-Logansport Tr. Co. - 31, 48, 61.
Lafayette St. Ry. - 28, 109.
Lakeside - 14.
Lakeside Line - 67, 83, 95.
Lakeside St. R.R. - 14, 26.
Last city car - 93.
"Lawton" - 36, 123.
Leesburg Rd. offices - 95.
Lewis Line - 14, 19, 45, 67, 71, 83, 95.
Lima, Ohio - 27.
Lima-Toledo Tr. Co. - 33.
Limited trains - 31.
Lindenwood Cemetery - 12.
"Little Turtle" - 128.
Logansport City Lines - 37, 47-49, 51, 60, 99, 101, 103, 149.
Logansport car barns - 36, 135.
Logansport Ry. Co. - 29, 101.
Logansport, Rochester & Northern Tr. Co. - 29, 103.
Lumbard, S. - 11.

McDonald, R. T. - 9, 26.
McGowan, H. - 29.
McGuire-Cummings Car Co. - 130.
McGuire trucks - 109.
McKinley, W. B. - 27.
McKinley Ave. - 81, 89, 130.
Main & Calhoun - 9, 14.
Maintenance cars - 143.
Marion, Ind. - 29, 53.
Marion, Bluffton & Eastern Tr. Co. - 33, 39, 43.
Marion & Bluffton Tr. Co. - 51, 53, 60, 81, 130, 145.
"Martha" - 36.
Maumee River - 11, 14.
Midland United - 60.
Mortgages - 11, 17.
Murdock, James and sons - 28-29.
Murdock syndicate - 28-29.
"Muzzle-loaders" - 110.

Nearsides - 110.
New York Central R.R. - 33, 56, 93.
Nickel Plate R.R. - 17, 105.
Ninth St. barn - 135.
Noble County Circuit Court - 11.
North Side High School - 88.
Northern Division - 51, 56, 60-61, 81, 125, 130, 135, 149.
Northern Indiana Power Co. - 60.

Office of Defense Transportation - 88-89.
Ohio - 29, 31, 60.
Ohio Electric Ry. - 29, 33, 51.
Oklahoma Rys. Co. - 128.
Old Orchard - 14.
Oxford Line - 71, 89.

P.A.Y.E. cars - 45, 110.
Park Board - 98.
Pearl Street - 53, 56.
Peckham trucks - 109.
Pennsylvania R.R. - 13, 32-33, 39, 44, 83.
Peru, Ind. - 29, 53, 60-61, 99, 101, 103, 135.
Peru City Lines - 29, 101.
Pinkerton detectives - 19.
Pittsburg, Ft. Wayne & Chicago R.R. - 13, 31.
Pontiac Line - 45, 67, 71, 88, 95.
Power houses - 14, 17, 36, 39, 75, 81.
Propane gas - 95, 147.
Public Service Co of Ind. - 60.
Purdue University - 110, 160.
Purdue University Test Car - 160.

Race Track Line - 19.
Rebuilding - 63.
Reservoir - 14, 75.
Riverview - 49.
Roanoke, Ind. - 51, 125.
Robison, M. S. - 17, 23, 25.
Robinson, F. deH. - 11, 25-26.
Rockhill House - 9.
Rockwell, H. C. - 25.
Rudisill School - 75.
Rule infractions - 42.

Safety islands - 67.
St. Joseph River - 14, 21, 75.
St. Louis Car Co. - 109, 113, 125.
St. Marys River - 11.
St. Petersburg, Fla. - 117.
Schoepf, W. K. - 29, 33.
Schoepf, McGowan Syndicate - 29, 31.
Scott, A. L. - 26.
"Second City Limited" - 128.
Securities and Exchange commissioners - 93.
Slattery, M. M. M. - 14.
South Barns (Baker St.) - 13, 44.
South Bend, Ind. - 53.
South Side High School - 83.
South Wayne Line - 45, 67, 71, 89.

Spencer Park - 38.
Springfield, Ohio - 33.
Spy Run Ave. Line - 19.
Spy Run Ave. plant - 14, 31, 39, 56, 75, 81, 89, 93, 130, 135.
Standard trucks - 113.
Stephenson, John, Car Co. - 105, 123.
State Highway Department - 83.
State School - 67, 93.
Street car parties - 18.
Strikes - 17-19, 89.
Summit City - 21.
Swift Park - 23.

Taylor Line - 45, 67, 89.
Tecumseh Trail Park - 38.
Terminal, passenger - 33, 53, 56.
Terre Haute, Indianapolis & Eastern Tr. Co. - 60.
Third St. Line - 67, 88, 95.
Thomson-Houston Co. - 18, 26.
Timken-Detroit trucks - 113.
Toledo, Ohio - 39.
Toledo & Chicago Interurban Ry. Co. - 33, 39, 43, 45, 81.
Toledo & Indiana Ry. - 39.
Traction-Light - 63, 93.
Trade & Labor Council - 19.
Transfer Corner - 13.
Trolley, bow - 143.
Trolley coaches - 83, 88, 95.
Twin Coach Co. - 121.
Turntable - 9, 12, 13.

"University Limited" - 128.
Union Traction Co. of Ind. - 31, 33, 36, 41-42, 51, 58, 60, 101, 125, 128.

Vestibules, closed - 107.

Wabash City Lines Co. - 60, 99, 135.
Wabash & Erie Canal - 9, 14, 21, 27.
Wabash-Logansport Traction Co. - 29.
Wabash Railroad - 29, 31, 83.
Wabash River - 31, 47, 99.
Wabash River Traction Co. - 29, 38, 99, 109.
"Wabash Valley Flyer" - 31, 51, 53, 128.
Wabash Valley Lines (See F.W. & W.V. Tr. Co.).
Wabash Valley Utilities - 51.
Walker, D. H. - 93, 98.
Warsaw, Ind. - 53.
Waterloo, Ind. - 33.
Webster substation - 81.
Western Ohio Ry. - 33.
West Main Line - 12, 17, 19, 67, 89.
West State Line - 83.
Wild Cat Creek - 47.
Wilson, D. - 42.
Winona Line - 101.
Work equipment - 141.
Wrecks (See accidents).

COLOPHON

FORT WAYNE'S TROLLEYS was produced in Fort Wayne, Indiana.

Title pages, chapter heads and sub heads were set in foundry type, dating from 1860 to 1900, by Herb Harnish from his unique and extensive collection of antique type faces.

All body copy was set by Graphic Typesetters, Inc., on the new A. T. F. photographic typesetting system, an extremely flexible photographic typesetting process utilizing a keyboard and photographic unit. The body is set in 10 point Spartan Book and 8 point Spartan Bold was used for the captions.

Precision Litho Plate, Inc. produced the litho negatives and plates.

Keefer Printing, Inc. printed the book on a 29 Miehle offset press using 70 lb. Consolith Opaque paper.

Binding and final work was completed by the Heckman Bindery Co. at North Manchester, Indiana.